Copyright © Panini UK Ltd
The Scottish Premier League name, initials and logo are all
Trade Marks of the Scottish Premier League Limited
Published by:
Panini UK Ltd, Panini House Coach & Horses Passage
The Pantiles, Tunbridge Wells
Kent TN2 5UJ

Edited by Iain King
Statistics by Forrest Robertson
Photographs by Allsport

Front Cover: (from left to right) Lorenzo Amoruso (Rangers),
Ian Durrant (Kilmarnock), John O'Neil (St Johnstone),
Henrik Larsson (Celtic)

Welcome to this fantastic review of season 1998-99. The first ever SPL Annual. The first season of the Bank of Scotland SPL was a record breaker for many reasons. More people attended games than ever before, Scottish matches were broadcast to over 120 countries worldwide, more cash was spent on players than in any previous season, and more young fans - the lifeblood of the game in Scotland - supported their star players through buying Panini stickers.

Youth development, bringing on the best young players Scotland has to offer, is at the heart of our efforts in the Bank of Scotland SPL. So it is great to see so many young fans building up their knowledge of the game, the clubs and the star personalities through the traditional Panini collection.

One of the best things about last season were the thousands of young supporters who mixed in a warm and friendly atmosphere at the Panini swapshop days. We are looking forward to making them bigger and better in the new season.

I am sure the 1999/2000 season will see even more great games, more goals and more skill than ever before.

We, at the SPL, are looking forward to the new season and we hope that all Panini collectors continue to enjoy their football.

Yours sincerely
Roger Mitchell
Chief Executive

THE CHAMPIONSHIP 1998/99

RANGERS regained their title and became the first champions of the new-look Scottish Premier League, finishing 6 points clear of their closest rival, Celtic. Although the Glasgow giants were rocked earlier in the season with a 5-1 defeat against their Old Firm adversary, they bounced right back with a bitterly fought 3-0 win at Celtic Park - a match which saw tempers boil and resulted in three players being red-carded.

Elsewhere, St. Johnstone's Sandy Clark and Killie's Bobby Williamson came through the season with flying colours - showing the nation that they had what it takes to match Dick Advocaat and Jozef Venglos.

As Hearts and Aberdeen under-achieved, Clark guided Saints to the League Cup Final, the final four of the Tennents Scottish Cup and then back into Europe for the first time in 28 YEARS. Williamson kept Killie on an upward curve and won a deserved bonus when his side also made the UEFA Cup through the Fair Play League. Now all that remains is for those four clubs to restore our Euro pride in season 1999-2000.

Final Table Scottish Premier League Final Tables Scottish

TEAM	PLAYED	HOME			GOALS		AWAY			GOALS		GD	PTS
		W	D	L	F	A	W	D	L	F	A		
Rangers	36	12	5	1	32	11	11	3	4	46	20	+47	77
Celtic	36	14	2	2	49	12	7	6	5	35	23	+49	71
St. Johnstone	36	8	7	3	24	18	7	5	6	15	20	+1	57
Kilmarnock	36	8	7	3	24	15	6	7	5	23	14	+18	56
Dundee	36	7	4	7	18	23	6	3	9	18	33	-20	46
Hearts	36	8	2	8	27	26	3	7	8	17	24	-6	42
Motherwell	36	6	5	7	20	31	4	6	8	15	23	-19	41
Aberdeen	36	6	4	8	24	35	4	3	11	19	36	-28	37
Dundee Utd.	36	2	8	8	13	22	6	2	10	24	26	-11	34
Dunfermline A	36	4	7	7	18	29	0	9	9	10	30	-31	28

SATURDAY, AUGUST 1ST, 1998
CELTIC 5 V. 0 DUNFERMLINE ATHLETIC
DUNDEE 0 V. 2 ABERDEEN
KILMARNOCK 2 V. 0 DUNDEE UNITED
MOTHERWELL 1 V. 0 ST. JOHNSTONE

SUNDAY, AUGUST 2ND, 1998
HEART OF MIDLOTHIAN 2 V. 1 RANGERS

SATURDAY, AUGUST 15TH, 1998
DUNFERMLINE ATHLETIC 2 V. 0 DUNDEE
RANGERS 2 V. 1 MOTHERWELL
ST. JOHNSTONE 0 V. 0 KILMARNOCK

SUNDAY, AUGUST 16TH, 1998
ABERDEEN 3 V. 2 CELTIC
DUNDEE UNITED 0 V. 0 HEART OF MIDLOTHIAN

SATURDAY, AUGUST 22ND, 1998
CELTIC 2 V. 1 DUNDEE UNITED
HEART OF MIDLOTHIAN 2 V. 0 ABERDEEN
KILMARNOCK 1 V. 3 RANGERS
MOTHERWELL 0 V. 0 DUNFERMLINE ATHLETIC

SUNDAY, AUGUST 23RD, 1998
DUNDEE 0 V. 1 ST. JOHNSTONE

SATURDAY, AUGUST 29TH, 1998
DUNDEE 1 V. 1 CELTIC
DUNFERMLINE ATHLETIC 1 V. 1 ABERDEEN
RANGERS 4 V. 0 ST. JOHNSTONE

SUNDAY, AUGUST 30TH, 1998
KILMARNOCK 3 V. 0 HEART OF MIDLOTHIAN
MOTHERWELL 1 V. 0 DUNDEE UNITED

SATURDAY, SEPTEMBER 12TH, 1998
ABERDEEN 1 V. 1 MOTHERWELL
CELTIC 1 V. 1 KILMARNOCK
DUNDEE UNITED 0 V. 0 RANGERS
HEART OF MIDLOTHIAN 0 V. 2 DUNDEE
ST. JOHNSTONE 1 V. 1 DUNFERMLINE ATHLETIC

SATURDAY, SEPTEMBER 19TH, 1998
DUNDEE 2 V. 2 DUNDEE UNITED
MOTHERWELL 2 V. 0 KILMARNOCK
ST. JOHNSTONE 2 V. 0 ABERDEEN

SUNDAY, SEPTEMBER 20TH, 1998
DUNFERMLINE ATHLETIC 1 V. 1 HEART OF MIDLOTHIAN
RANGERS 0 V. 0 CELTIC

WEDNESDAY, SEPTEMBER 23RD, 1998
ABERDEEN 1 V. 1 RANGERS
CELTIC 0 V. 1 ST. JOHNSTONE
DUNDEE UNITED 1 V. 1 DUNFERMLINE ATHLETIC
HEART OF MIDLOTHIAN 3 V. 0 MOTHERWELL
KILMARNOCK 2 V. 1 DUNDEE

SATURDAY, SEPTEMBER 26TH, 1998
CELTIC 1 V. 1 HEART OF MIDLOTHIAN
DUNDEE 1 V. 0 MOTHERWELL
DUNFERMLINE ATHLETIC 0 V. 2 RANGERS
ST. JOHNSTONE 1 V. 3 DUNDEE UNITED

SUNDAY, SEPTEMBER 27TH, 1998
ABERDEEN 0 V. 1 KILMARNOCK

SATURDAY, OCTOBER 3RD, 1998
KILMARNOCK 0 V. 0 DUNFERMLINE ATHLETIC
MOTHERWELL 1 V. 2 CELTIC

SUNDAY, OCTOBER 4TH, 1998
DUNDEE UNITED 1 V. 0 ABERDEEN
HEART OF MIDLOTHIAN 1 V. 1 ST. JOHNSTONE
RANGERS 1 V. 0 DUNDEE

SATURDAY, OCTOBER 17TH, 1998
ABERDEEN 2 V. 2 DUNDEE
DUNDEE UNITED 0 V. 2 KILMARNOCK
DUNFERMLINE ATHLETIC 2 V. 2 CELTIC
RANGERS 3 V. 0 HEART OF MIDLOTHIAN
ST. JOHNSTONE 5 V. 0 MOTHERWELL

SATURDAY, OCTOBER 24TH, 1998
CELTIC 2 V. 0 ABERDEEN
HEART OF MIDLOTHIAN 0 V. 1 DUNDEE UNITED
KILMARNOCK 2 V. 2 ST. JOHNSTONE

TUESDAY, OCTOBER 27TH, 1998
DUNDEE 1 V. 0 DUNFERMLINE ATHLETIC
MOTHERWELL 1 V. 0 RANGERS

SATURDAY, OCTOBER 31ST, 1998
DUNDEE 1 V. 0 HEART OF MIDLOTHIAN
DUNFERMLINE ATHLETIC 1 V. 1 ST. JOHNSTONE
KILMARNOCK 2 V. 0 CELTIC
MOTHERWELL 2 V. 2 ABERDEEN
RANGERS 2 V. 1 DUNDEE UNITED

SATURDAY, NOVEMBER 7TH, 1998
ABERDEEN 2 V. 1 DUNFERMLINE ATHLETIC
DUNDEE UNITED 2 V. 2 MOTHERWELL
CELTIC 6 V. 1 DUNDEE

HEART OF MIDLOTHIAN 2 V. 1 KILMARNOCK

SUNDAY, NOVEMBER 8TH, 1998
ST. JOHNSTONE 0 V. 7 RANGERS

SATURDAY, NOVEMBER 14TH, 1998
DUNDEE 1 V. 1 KILMARNOCK
MOTHERWELL 3 V. 2 HEART OF MIDLOTHIAN
RANGERS 2 V. 1 ABERDEEN
ST. JOHNSTONE 2 V. 1 CELTIC

SUNDAY, NOVEMBER 15TH, 1998
DUNFERMLINE ATHLETIC 2 V. 1 DUNDEE UNITED

SATURDAY, NOVEMBER 21ST, 1998
ABERDEEN 0 V. 1 ST. JOHNSTONE
CELTIC 5 V. 1 RANGERS
HEART OF MIDLOTHIAN 2 V. 1 DUNFERMLINE ATHLETIC
KILMARNOCK 0 V. 0 MOTHERWELL

SUNDAY, NOVEMBER 22ND, 1998
DUNDEE UNITED 0 V. 1 DUNDEE

SATURDAY, NOVEMBER 28TH, 1998
ABERDEEN 0 V. 3 DUNDEE UNITED
CELTIC 2 V. 0 MOTHERWELL
DUNFERMLINE ATHLETIC 0 V. 3 KILMARNOCK

SATURDAY, DECEMBER 5TH, 1998
DUNDEE UNITED 1 V. 1 ST. JOHNSTONE
KILMARNOCK 4 V. 0 ABERDEEN
RANGERS 1 V. 1 DUNFERMLINE ATHLETIC

SUNDAY, DECEMBER 6TH, 1998
HEART OF MIDLOTHIAN 2 V. 1 CELTIC

WEDNESDAY, DECEMBER 9TH, 1998
ST. JOHNSTONE 1 V. 1 HEART OF MIDLOTHIAN

SATURDAY, DECEMBER 12TH, 1998
ABERDEEN 2 V. 0 HEART OF MIDLOTHIAN
DUNDEE UNITED 1 V. 1 CELTIC
DUNFERMLINE ATHLETIC 1 V. 1 MOTHERWELL
RANGERS 1 V. 0 KILMARNOCK
ST. JOHNSTONE 1 V. 1 DUNDEE

WEDNESDAY, DECEMBER 16TH, 1998
MOTHERWELL 2 V. 1 DUNDEE

SATURDAY, DECEMBER 19TH, 1998
CELTIC 5 V. 0 DUNFERMLINE ATHLETIC
DUNDEE 1 V. 2 ABERDEEN
HEART OF MIDLOTHIAN 2 V. 3 RANGERS
MOTHERWELL 1 V. 1 ST. JOHNSTONE

SUNDAY, DECEMBER 20TH, 1998
KILMARNOCK 2 V. 0 DUNDEE UNITED

SATURDAY, DECEMBER 26TH, 1998
DUNFERMLINE ATHLETIC 1 V. 2 ABERDEEN
KILMARNOCK 1 V. 0 HEART OF MIDLOTHIAN
MOTHERWELL 2 V. 0 DUNDEE UNITED
RANGERS 1 V. 0 ST. JOHNSTONE

SUNDAY, DECEMBER 27TH, 1998
DUNDEE 0 V. 3 CELTIC

TUESDAY, DECEMBER 29TH, 1998
ABERDEEN 1 V. 1 MOTHERWELL
ST. JOHNSTONE 1 V. 1 DUNFERMLINE ATHLETIC

WEDNESDAY, DECEMBER 30TH, 1998
DUNDEE UNITED 1 V. 2 RANGERS
HEART OF MIDLOTHIAN 1 V. 2 DUNDEE

FRIDAY, JANUARY 1ST, 1999
MOTHERWELL 1 V. 2 KILMARNOCK

SATURDAY, JANUARY 2ND, 1999
DUNDEE 1 V. 3 DUNDEE UNITED
DUNFERMLINE ATHLETIC 0 V. 0 HEART OF MIDLOTHIAN
ST. JOHNSTONE 4 V. 1 ABERDEEN

SUNDAY, JANUARY 3RD, 1999
RANGERS 2 V. 2 CELTIC

WEDNESDAY, JANUARY 27TH, 1999
DUNDEE 0 V. 4 RANGERS

SATURDAY, JANUARY 30TH, 1999
ABERDEEN 2 V. 4 RANGERS
CELTIC 5 V. 0 ST. JOHNSTONE
DUNDEE UNITED 1 V. 1 DUNFERMLINE ATHLETIC
HEART OF MIDLOTHIAN 0 V. 2 MOTHERWELL
KILMARNOCK 0 V. 0 DUNDEE

SATURDAY, FEBRUARY 6TH, 1999
ABERDEEN 2 V. 1 KILMARNOCK
CELTIC 3 V. 0 HEART OF MIDLOTHIAN
DUNDEE 1 V. 0 MOTHERWELL
ST. JOHNSTONE 1 V. 0 DUNDEE UNITED

SUNDAY, FEBRUARY 7TH, 1999
DUNFERMLINE ATHLETIC 0 V. 3 RANGERS

WEDNESDAY, FEBRUARY 17TH, 1999
CELTIC 1 V. 0 KILMARNOCK

SATURDAY, FEBRUARY 20TH, 1999
DUNDEE UNITED 3 V. 0 ABERDEEN
HEART OF MIDLOTHIAN 0 V. 1 ST. JOHNSTONE
RANGERS 6 V. 1 DUNDEE

SUNDAY, FEBRUARY 21ST, 1999
MOTHERWELL 1 V. 7 CELTIC

SATURDAY, FEBRUARY 27TH, 1999
CELTIC 2 V. 1 DUNDEE UNITED
DUNDEE 0 V. 1 ST. JOHNSTONE
HEART OF MIDLOTHIAN 0 V. 2 ABERDEEN
MOTHERWELL 1 V. 1 DUNFERMLINE ATHLETIC

SUNDAY, FEBRUARY 28TH, 1999
KILMARNOCK 0 V. 5 RANGERS

SATURDAY, MARCH 6TH, 1999
KILMARNOCK 2 V. 0 DUNFERMLINE ATHLETIC

SUNDAY, MARCH 14TH, 1999
ABERDEEN 1 V. 5 CELTIC
DUNFERMLINE ATHLETIC 2 V. 0 DUNDEE
RANGERS 2 V. 1 MOTHERWELL
ST. JOHNSTONE 0 V. 1 KILMARNOCK

SATURDAY, MARCH 20TH, 1999
DUNDEE 2 V. 0 HEART OF MIDLOTHIAN
DUNFERMLINE ATHLETIC 1 V. 0 ST. JOHNSTONE
MOTHERWELL 1 V. 1 ABERDEEN
RANGERS 0 V. 1 DUNDEE UNITED

SUNDAY, MARCH 21ST, 1999
KILMARNOCK 0 V. 0 CELTIC

SATURDAY, APRIL 3RD, 1999
ABERDEEN 3 V. 1 DUNFERMLINE ATHLETIC
CELTIC 5 V. 0 DUNDEE
DUNDEE UNITED 0 V. 3 MOTHERWELL
HEART OF MIDLOTHIAN 2 V. 2 KILMARNOCK
ST. JOHNSTONE 3 V. 1 RANGERS

TUESDAY, APRIL 6TH, 1999
DUNDEE UNITED 1 V. 3 HEART OF MIDLOTHIAN

SATURDAY, APRIL 10TH, 1999
KILMARNOCK 4 V. 2 ABERDEEN
MOTHERWELL 1 V. 2 DUNDEE

WEDNESDAY, APRIL 14TH, 1999
HEART OF MIDLOTHIAN 2 V. 4 CELTIC
RANGERS 1 V. 0 DUNFERMLINE ATHLETIC

SATURDAY, APRIL 17TH, 1999
ABERDEEN 0 V. 4 DUNDEE UNITED
CELTIC 1 V. 0 MOTHERWELL
DUNFERMLINE ATHLETIC 0 V. 6 KILMARNOCK
ST. JOHNSTONE 0 V. 0 HEART OF MIDLOTHIAN

SUNDAY, APRIL 18TH, 1999
DUNDEE 1 V. 1 RANGERS

TUESDAY, APRIL 20TH, 1999
DUNDEE UNITED 0 V. 1 ST. JOHNSTONE

SATURDAY, APRIL 24TH, 1999
DUNDEE 2 V. 1 KILMARNOCK
DUNFERMLINE ATHLETIC 2 V. 2 DUNDEE UNITED
MOTHERWELL 0 V. 4 HEART OF MIDLOTHIAN
ST. JOHNSTONE 1 V. 0 CELTIC

SUNDAY, APRIL 25TH, 1999
RANGERS 3 V. 1 ABERDEEN

SATURDAY, MAY 1ST, 1999
ABERDEEN 1 V. 0 ST. JOHNSTONE
DUNDEE UNITED 0 V. 2 DUNDEE
KILMARNOCK 1 V. 0 MOTHERWELL

SUNDAY, MAY 2ND, 1999
CELTIC 0 V. 3 RANGERS

MONDAY, MAY 3RD, 1999
HEART OF MIDLOTHIAN 2 V. 0 DUNFERMLINE ATHLETIC

SATURDAY, MAY 8TH, 1999
ABERDEEN 1 V. 0 DUNDEE
DUNDEE UNITED 0 V. 0 KILMARNOCK
DUNFERMLINE ATHLETIC 1 V. 2 CELTIC
ST. JOHNSTONE 0 V. 0 MOTHERWELL

SUNDAY, MAY 9TH, 1999
RANGERS 0 V. 0 HEART OF MIDLOTHIAN

SATURDAY, MAY 15TH, 1999
CELTIC 3 V. 2 ABERDEEN
DUNDEE 3 V. 1 DUNFERMLINE ATHLETIC
HEART OF MIDLOTHIAN 4 V. 1 DUNDEE UNITED
KILMARNOCK 1 V. 1 ST. JOHNSTONE
MOTHERWELL 1 V. 5 RANGERS

SUNDAY, MAY 23RD, 1999
ABERDEEN 2 V. 5 HEART OF MIDLOTHIAN
DUNDEE UNITED 1 V. 2 CELTIC
DUNFERMLINE ATHLETIC 1 V. 2 MOTHERWELL
RANGERS 1 V. 1 KILMARNOCK
ST. JOHNSTONE 1 V. 0 DUNDEE

HENRIK LARSSON WINS AWARDS DOUBLE

CELTIC superstar Henrik Larsson was voted Player of the Year by fellow professionals and the Scottish Football Writers' Association.

Personal joy was tempered with the disappointment of a trophyless season for Celtic, and Henrik said: "At this club I know that it is the team who must win prizes."

ScottishLeagueChampions

HONOURS LIST

DIVISION ONE					
1890/91	Dumbarton/Rangers	1912/13	Rangers	1935/36	Celtic
1891/92	Dumbarton	1913/14	Celtic	1936/37	Rangers
1892/93	Celtic	1914/15	Celtic	1937/38	Celtic
1893/94	Celtic	1915/16	Celtic	1938/39	Rangers
1894/95	Heart of Midlothian	1916/17	Celtic	1939/40	(No Competition)
1895/96	Celtic	1917/18	Rangers	1940/41	(No Competition)
1896/97	Heart of Midlothian	1918/19	Celtic	1941/42	(No Competition)
1897/98	Celtic	1919/20	Rangers	1942/43	(No Competition)
1898/99	Rangers	1920/21	Rangers	1943/44	(No Competition)
1899/0	Rangers	1921/22	Celtic	1944/45	(No Competition)
1900/1	Rangers	1922/23	Rangers	1945/46	(No Competition)
1901/2	Rangers	1923/24	Rangers	1946/47	Rangers
1902/3	Hibernian	1924/25	Rangers	1947/48	Hibernian
1903/4	Third Lanark	1925/26	Celtic	1948/49	Rangers
1904/5	Celtic (after play-off)	1926/27	Rangers	1949/50	Rangers
1905/6	Celtic	1927/28	Rangers	1950/51	Hibernian
1906/7	Celtic	1928/29	Rangers	1951/52	Hibernian
1907/8	Celtic	1929/30	Rangers	1952/53	Rangers ✖
1908/9	Celtic	1930/31	Rangers	1953/54	Celtic
1909/10	Celtic	1931/32	Motherwell	1954/55	Aberdeen
1910/11	Rangers	1932/33	Rangers	1955/56	Rangers
1911/12	Rangers	1933/34	Rangers	1956/57	Rangers
		1934/35	Rangers	1957/58	Heart of Midlothian

1958/59	Rangers	1979/80	Aberdeen
1959/60	Heart of Midlothian	1980/81	Celtic
1960/61	Rangers	1981/82	Celtic
1961/62	Dundee	1982/83	Dundee United
1962/63	Rangers	1983/84	Aberdeen
1963/64	Rangers	1984/85	Aberdeen
1964/65	Kilmarnock	1985/86	Celtic ❑ ○
1965/66	Celtic	1986/87	Rangers ○
1966/67	Celtic	1987/88	Celtic ○
1967/68	Celtic	1988/89	Rangers ▲
1968/69	Celtic	1989/90	Rangers ▲
1969/70	Celtic	1990/91	Rangers ▲
1970/71	Celtic	1991/92	Rangers ▲
1971/72	Celtic	1992/93	Rangers
1972/73	Celtic	1993/94	Rangers
1973/74	Celtic	1994/95	Rangers ●
1974/75	Rangers	1995/96	Rangers ●
		1996/97	Rangers ●
PREMIER DIVISION		1997/98	Celtic ●
1975/76	Rangers		
1976/77	Celtic	**BANK OF SCOTLAND**	
1977/78	Rangers	**SCOTTISH PREMIER LEAGUE**	
1978/79	Celtic	1998/99	Rangers

✖ Champions on goal average   ○ Competition known as Fine Fare League   ● Competition known as Bell's League Championship
❑ Champions on goal difference   ▲ Competition known as B & Q League

8

BANK OF SCOTLAND SPL

THE TEAM
of the Year

SPL backers Bank of Scotland sparked a whole new footballing debate in the country this season by bringing in the selection of the Team of the Season. It was voted for by the Scottish Football Writers' Association who chose Rangers' Dick Advocaat as their Manager of the Year to boss it.

Goalkeeper

Gordon Marshall (Kilmarnock)

EQUALLED the club's shut-out record and signed a new long-term deal that will keep him at Rugby Park until he is 38. Marsh reflected: "I think as I have got older I have improved, especially organising a defence that was proud to be the best in the SPL."

Defenders

Sergio Porrini (Rangers)

THE former Juventus defender found superb consistency and could go only look back on one black mark in a Treble season. He sighed: "I still wish I could go back to the UEFA Cup defeat in Parma and avoid my red card. More than anything I wanted to prove a point in Italy."

Lorenzo Amoruso (Rangers)

MADE a gutsy journey back from some erratic early season form to become a colossus at the heart of the Gers defence. And Amo rapped: "Next term is the start of our three-year plan to win the European Cup - I firmly believe that."

Kevin McGowne (Kilmarnock)

ANOTHER Killie star whose brilliant form in the meanest defence in the league won him a new four-year deal from Bobby Williamson. McGowne has developed late into a superb defender and he said: "I'm delighted to be in the team of the year and there's even been talk of a call-up to the Scotland squad. That has to be my aim for next season."

Tom Boyd (Celtic)

OUTSTANDING for club and country as he hoisted his caps tally to 65 and beat the total of his hero Danny McGrain. Boyd said: "Only Kenny Dalglish, Jim Leighton, Alex McLeish and Paul McStay have more caps now and I'm proud of that."

Midfielders

Paul Lambert (Celtic)

TRANSFORMED as a player since he switched from Motherwell to Borussia Dortmund and now Celtic enjoy the class of a European Cup winner. And Paul insisted: "I've got no regrets about coming home. Celtic are as big as Dortmund, we just need the Euro success that they had."

Ian Durrant (Kilmarnock)

REJUVENATED as a player after two wasted years at the end of 14 seasons at Rangers and was ever-present for Killie. He said: "The high point of it all for me was simply coming through it unscathed and winning back my Scotland place."

Giovanni van Bronckhorst (Rangers)

BROUGHT to Scotland by his mentor Dick Advocaat and justified the £5million price tag with a superb first season. Delighted his boss signed a new deal and he promised: "I know that we can only get stronger under him next season."

Neil McCann (Rangers)

ADVOCAAT'S masterstroke signing for £1.6million from Hearts mid-season. McCann's undoubted skills were matched with growing confidence as his performances shone at a bigger club. Celtic fan as a kid, but reasoned: "They could have bought me and they didn't. I know where my allegiance lies."

Forwards

Rod Wallace (Rangers)

STARTED his season with a goal at Hearts and finished it with the winner in the Tennents Scottish Cup Final triumph over Celtic. He reckons the team lunching together under Advocaat's rule was a key to success and said: "It built an unbreakable team spirit."

Henrik Larsson (Celtic)

HENRIK LARSSON'S 38 goal season may have dried up in the closing weeks but by then he'd carried a team on his shoulders too long. Happy in Scotland and committed to Celtic until 2003 he revelled in Sweden's Euro 2000 supremacy over England and said: "I hate their sniping."

ANY Old Firm clash is a date of significance for the fans who follow Scottish football's superpowers but, May 29th 1999 will now be written into the history books at Rangers. They clinched the Tennents Scottish Cup with a Rod Wallace goal and the 1-0 victory brought them their sixth Treble in 126 years. It was a day when two players confirmed their growing status in Gers' folklore. Skipper Lorenzo Amoruso - booed by his OWN fans earlier that season - was the deserved Man of the Match. And Wallace's 27th strike of the season left him to reveal: "When you win one trophy it just makes you want to keep lifting them. Dick Advocaat is keen to win every trophy possible and that feeling flows through everyone."

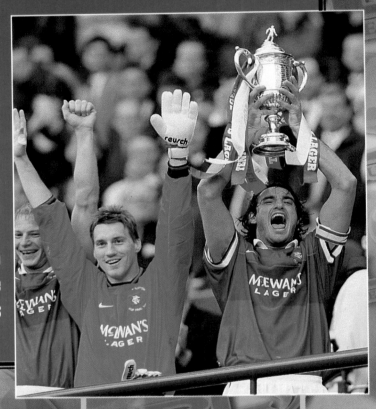

RANGERSRANGERSRANGERSR

1	Klos
2	Porrini
3	Amoruso – *capt.*
4	Hendry
5	Vidmar
6	McCann
7	McInnes
8	Van Bronckhorst
9	Wallace
10	Amato
11	Albertz

SUBSTITUTES
Ferguson (15) for McCann 67 minutes
Kanchelskis (14) for Porrini 77 minutes
Wilson (16) for Amato 89 minutes

YELLOW CARDS
Wallace

CELTICCELTICCELTICCELTICCELTIC

1	Gould
2	Boyd – *capt.*
3	Mahe
6	Stubbs
7	Larsson
11	Wieghorst
14	Lambert
17	Annoni
20	Blinker
25	Moravcik
35	Mjallby

SUBSTITUTES
Johnson (12) for Annoni 60 minutes
O'Donnell (10) for Mahe 79 minutes
Kerr (21) – not used.

YELLOW CARDS
Boyd / Wieghorst / Blinker / Mjallby

REFEREE
Hugh Dallas (Motherwell)

ASSISTANT REFEREES
John Love & David Doig

REFEREE SUPERVISOR
Kenny Clark

TOP GOAL SCORERS

THE TOP SCORER
OF THE BHOYS
Henrik Larsson
38 goals

CELTIC'S pain over relinquishing the championship was salved by the news that Henrik Larsson will be at the club until 2003. Slick Swede Larsson's skill and stealth has brought a sackful of goals and he stressed: "I played in the World Cup Finals for my country and that's a dream come true. I played in the semi-finals of a European competition with Feyenoord. Now going a long way in Europe with Celtic is one of the ambitions I hope to achieve during the next four years."

PLAYER	TEAM	LEAGUE	SCOTTISH CUPS	LEAGUE CUP	EUROPEAN CUP	TOTAL
Henrik Larsson	Celtic	29	5	-	4	38
Rod Wallace	Rangers	19	3	2	3	27
Billy Dodds	Dundee Utd	16	1	3	-	20
Jorg Albertz	Rangers	11	1	3	4	19
Jonatan Johansson	Rangers	8	3	1	5	17
Eoin Jess	Aberdeen	14	0	0	0	14
Gary McSwegan	Hearts	11	0	1	0	12
						(4 for Dundee Utd)
Neil McCann	Rangers	8	3	0	1	12
						(4 for Hearts)
Jim Hamilton	Aberdeen	7	1	1	2	11
						(10 for Hearts)
Derek Adams	Motherwell	6	0	5	0	11
						(8 for Ross County)

THE TOP SCORER
OF THE GERS
Rod Wallace
27 goals

ROD WALLACE came to Ibrox for free - and he has cashed in with the best goalscoring season of his life, capped by the Cup Final winner.

He has now won title medals on BOTH sides of the border after his 1992 triumph with Leeds United in England. With Stephane Guivarc'h, Gabriel Amato and Jonaton Johansson sharing the striking duties, Rod had to prove to Dick Advocaat that he was the main man.

Rod said: "The season I won the league with Leeds was one of the best years of my life - and this year has been right up there."

THE TOP SCORER
OF THE ARABS
Billy Dodds
20 goals

BILLY DODDS suffered a nerve-jangling battle against relegation - despite having the best season of his career to date. Amidst all the dark days at Tannadice the Scotland striker stood out like a beacon as the only real ray of hope for United fans. Billy said: "It hurt when I became surplus to Alex Miller's requirements, at Pittodrie. But it's a constant process maturing as a player and all my life I have enjoyed proving people wrong."

ABERDEEN

ABERDEEN FOOTBALL CLUB (1903)

PITTODRIE has become a graveyard for managers as the club - like New Firm rivals Dundee United - struggle to live up to their predecessors. Willie Miller, Roy Aitken and then this season Alex Miller and Paul Hegarty have all tried and failed to emulate the success of Alex Smith and Jocky Scott who brought both Cups north to the Granite City in 1990. Chairman Stewart Milne now faces a critical season with the club at a crossroads and Dane Ebbe Skovdahl must find the route back to greatness. Rebuilding of the squad is much-needed and the depths of the Dons' fall from grace is shown in a fair assessment of their targets for the season from the honest Hegarty. He tooked over as caretaker from the axed Alex Miller in mid-season and when he wasn't given the job full-time in May he said: "I did what I was asked to do because I didn't want to be the first manager to take them down. Wanting to stay out of the First Division wasn't negative, it was REALISTIC."

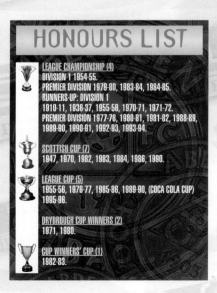

HONOURS LIST

LEAGUE CHAMPIONSHIP (4)
DIVISION 1 1954-55.
PREMIER DIVISION 1979-80, 1983-84, 1984-85.
RUNNERS-UP: DIVISION 1
1910-11, 1936-37, 1955-56, 1970-71, 1971-72.
PREMIER DIVISION 1977-78, 1980-81, 1981-82, 1988-89,
1989-90, 1990-91, 1992-93, 1993-94.

SCOTTISH CUP (7)
1947, 1970, 1982, 1983, 1984, 1986, 1990.

LEAGUE CUP (5)
1955-56, 1976-77, 1985-86, 1989-90, (COCA COLA CUP)
1995-96.

DRYBROUGH CUP WINNERS (2)
1971, 1980.

CUP WINNERS' CUP (1)
1982-83.

THE DEFENDER OF THE DONS
Derek Whyte

MY HIGH FIVE ➡

FAVOURITE BAND: U2
BEST MOVIE: The Godfather Trilogy.
OTHER TEAM: Celtic, I spent so long there they'll always be in my heart.
PIN-UP: Meg Ryan, no contest really.
HOBBY AWAY FROM FOOTBALL: My daughter Chelsea and son Cruise take up all my time.

PLAYER LIST

name	season 98-99 app	sub	goals
Jim Leighton	22		
Mark Perry	32	4	
Derek White	35		
Nigel Pepper	7	+3	
John Inglis	15	+1	1
Gary Smith	30		
Craig Hignett (to Nov. 98)	13		2
Jim Hamilton (from Apr. 99)	6	+1	1
Eoin Jess	36		14
Mike Newell	14	+9	2
Billy Dodds (to Sep. 98)	6		
Andreas Mayer (from Jan. 99)	13		2
Ilian Kiriakov	17	+5	
Andy Dow	22	+3	
Derek Stillie	9		
Paul Bernard	8	+1	1
Russell Anderson	13	+3	
Jamie Buchan	19	+3	2
David Rowson	19	+3	
Ricky Gillies	4	+7	
Darren Young	11		
Dennis Wyness	8	+6	1
Darren Young	1	+3	
Michael Hart	4	+9	
Ryan Esson	0		
Russell Duncan	0		
Stuart McCaffrey	0		
Robbie Winters	28		12
Baldur Bett	1		
Iain Good	0	+1	
Darren Mackie	0		
Alex Notman	0	+2	
Fergus Teirnan	0		
Tony Warner	6		

HOME GROUND

PITTODRIE STADIUM

PITTODRIE STREET, Aberdeen, AB24 5QH. Tel. (01224) 650400

CAPACITY

22,199 (ALL SEATED)

Pitch Dimensions

109 YDS X 72 YDS.

Ticket Office

(01224) 632328

THE MANAGER

Ebbe Skovdahl

DANE Ebbe faces a huge task after making his name with Brondby in his homeland. And he has moved quickly to enlist local knowledge as he bids to bring respectability back to Pittodrie. The appointment of his countryman, Rangers' coach Tommy Moller Nielsen, as his No.2 is a wise one. (Replaced Paul Hegarty June 1999).

TEAM LINE-UP

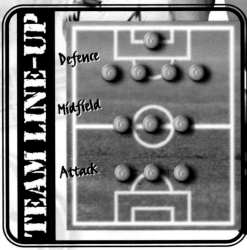

Defence

Midfield

Attack

HOME ↑
AND
↓ AWAY

THE HERO
OF THE DONS
Robbie Winters

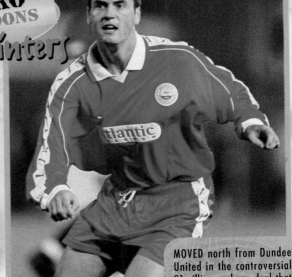

10-YEAR RECORD

Season	Division	Pts	Final Pos.
1989/90	P	44	2
1990/91	P	53	2
1991/92	P	48	6
1992/93	P	64	2
1993/94	P	55	2
1994/95	P	41	9
1995/96	P	55	3
1996/97	P	44	6
1997/98	P	39	6
1998/99	P	37	8

MOVED north from Dundee United in the controversial £1million package deal that took fans' favourite Billy Dodds to Tannadice. Robbie took his time to adapt in a struggling team but his pace looks a vital asset now and his late season form was rewarded with a Scotland call-up for the brilliant friendly win in Germany.

THE FOREIGNER
OF THE DONS
Andreas Mayer

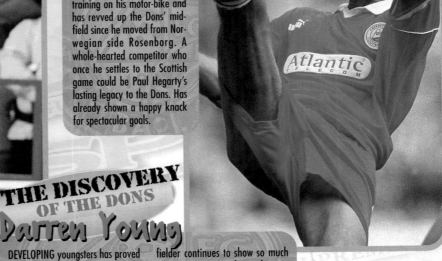

DESIGNER stubble, drives to training on his motor-bike and has revved up the Dons' midfield since he moved from Norwegian side Rosenborg. A whole-hearted competitor who once he settles to the Scottish game could be Paul Hegarty's lasting legacy to the Dons. Has already shown a happy knack for spectacular goals.

THE DISCOVERY
OF THE DONS
Darren Young

DEVELOPING youngsters has proved difficult at Dons as the club stumble from one crisis to the next. But through it all this tenacious midfielder continues to show so much promise. Strong and crunching in the tackle for one so slight and has good composure in possession.

THE BEST OF THE DONS

Eoin Jess

PLAYER PROFILE

THEY said he'd never fulfilled his potential and they said he was too inconsistent. But you could never throw those accusations at Eoin Jess this season. He shone through whether up front or in midfield and there's only one certainty next season - with good support he can only improve further.

HEIGHT	WEIGHT	Date of Birth	Place of Birth
5ft 9ins	11st 9lbs	13/12/70	Aberdeen

CARER:	SEASON	CLUB	APP.	GOALS
	87-96	Aberdeen	201	50
	96-97	Coventry City	39	1
	97-99	Aberdeen	71	24

INTERNATIONAL CAPS

APP.	GOALS
15	1

MIDFIELDER

SQUAD NUMBER: 8

THEDONS THEDONS THEDONS THEDONS THEDONS THEDONS THEDONS THEDONS THEDONS THEDONS

CELTIC

DR JOZEF VENGLOS was a controversial appointment for Celtic after the one-season reign of Wim Jansen brought the title back to Paradise. The scholarly Slovak was well-liked and did mastermind a 5-1 win over Rangers, the club's biggest Old Firm triumph since 1966. But the bottom line for the Glasgow giants is trophies and he surrendered the lot to Rangers. Now he will remain with the club as European talent scout as another new era begins under Director of Football Operations Kenny Dalglish and head coach John Barnes. Venglos, now 63, insisted: "There's no disappointment from me because it's important for the club to think in the long term." Now Dalglish - a legend with the club as a player before he moved south to Liverpool in 1977 - knows what he must do. He stressed: "Rangers got the trophies because they deserved them and it's important for us to now get to their level. We won't shout our mouths off but we want to deliver that sort of success."

HONOURS LIST

LEAGUE CHAMPIONSHIP (36)
DIVISION 1 1892-93, 1893-94, 1895-96, 1897-98, 1904-05, 1905-06, 1906-07, 1907-08, 1908-09, 1909-10, 1913-14, 1914-15, 1915-16, 1916-17, 1918-19, 1921-22, 1925-26, 1935-36, 1937-38, 1953-54, 1965-66, 1966-67, 1967-68, 1968-69, 1969-70, 1970-71, 1971-72, 1972-73, 1973-74, PREMIER DIVISION 1976-77, 1978-79, 1980-81, 1981-82, 1985-86, 1987-88, 1997-98.

SCOTTISH CUP (30)
1892, 1899, 1900, 1904, 1907, 1908, 1911, 1912, 1914, 1923, 1925, 1927, 1931, 1933, 1937, 1951, 1954, 1965, 1967, 1969, 1971, 1972, 1974, 1975, 1977, 1980, 1985, 1988, 1989, 1995.

LEAGUE CUP (10)
1956-57, 1957-58, 1965-66, 1966-67, 1967-68, 1968-69, 1969-70, 1974-75, 1982-83, 1997-98.

EUROPEAN CUP (1)
1966-67. RUNNERS-UP: 1970.

CUP WINNERS' CUP
1963-64 SEMI-FINALS, 1965-66 SEMI-FINALS

THE PLAYMAKER OF THE BHOYS
Regi Blinker

MY HIGH FIVE

FAVOURITE BAND: Busta Rhymes, rap at its best.
BEST MOVIE: The Usual Suspects.
OTHER TEAM: Barcelona, they had Cruyff and I love the Nou Camp.
PIN-UP: Letitia Casta - she's a supermodel.
HOBBY AWAY FROM FOOTBALL: I'm a shopaholic for clothes and stuff.

PLAYER LIST

name	season 98-99 app	sub	goals
Jonathan Gould	28		
Tom Boyd	31		
Stephane Mahe	24		
Jackie McNamara	15	+1	
Marc Rieper	7		
Alan Stubbs	22	+1	1
Henrik Larsson	35		28
Craig Burley	20	+1	9
Harald Brattbakk	16	+9	5
Phil O'Donnell	14	+2	3
Morten Wieghorst	5	+2	
Tommy Johnson	2		3
Simon Donnelly	21	+3	5
Paul Lambert	33		1
Darren Jackson	4	+2	
David Hannah	5	+4	
Enrico Annoni	9	+5	
Tosh McKinlay	11	+7	
Malky Mackay	1		1
Regi Blinker	13	+2	4
Stewart Kerr	4		
Brian McLaughlin	0		
Andy McCondichie	1		
Colin Healy	2	+1	
Lubomir Moravcik	14		6
John Paul McBride	0	+1	
Mark Burchill	5	+16	8
Barry Elliot	0		
Vidar Riseth	26	+1	3
Tony Warner	3		
Johan Mjallby	17		1
Mark Viduka	8	+1	5
Barry John Corr	0	+1	
Scott Marshall	1	+1	

HOME GROUND

CELTIC PARK	GLASGOW, G40 3RE TEL. (0141) 556 2611
CAPACITY	60,294 (All Seated)
Pitch Dimensions	120 YDS X 74 YDS
Ticket Services	(0141) 551 4223

CREDIT CARD HOTLINE (0141) 551 8653/4

THE MANAGER

John Barnes

HAS all the credentials to be a top coach after a glittering playing career that brought a host of honours with Liverpool and 79 international caps for England. And he insists: "I feel my whole career to date has been an apprenticeship for coaching." (Replaced Dr. Jozef Venglos June 1999)

TEAM LINE-UP

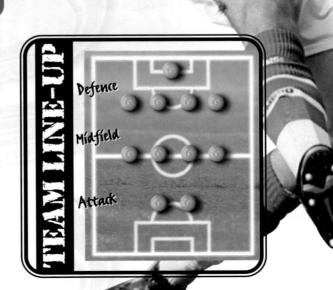

Defence

Midfield

Attack

HOME ⬆
AND
AWAY ⬇

WHEN THE GOALS WERE SCORED

	0-15	16-30	31-45	46-60	61-75	79-90
Celtic	11	11	13	16	17	16

	League	Cup	Europe	Total
Henrik Larsson	28	5	4	37
Craig Burley	9			9
Harald Brattbakk	5	1	2	8
Mark Viduka	5	3		8
Mark Burchill	8			8

10-YEAR RECORD

Season	Division	Pts	Final Pos.
1989/90	P	34	5
1990/91	P	41	3
1991/92	P	62	3
1992/93	P	60	3
1993/94	P	50	4
1994/95	P	51	4
1995/96	P	83	2
1996/97	P	75	2
1997/98	P	74	1
1998/99	P	71	2

TRUE OR FALSE?

1. Tommy Gemmell scored for Celtic in both their European Cup Final appearances, true or false?

2. The 1995 Tennents Scottish Cup was the ONLY trophy Paul McStay lifted as captain, true or false?

3. Craig Burley is the club's record signing at £2.5m, true or false?

4. Mark Viduka scored for Croatia Zagreb against Celtic before he joined the club, true or false?

5. Jorge Cadete never scored against Rangers during his Celtic days, true or false?

(ANSWERS ON PAGE 60)

THE BEST
OF THE BHOYS
Henrik Larsson

THE CELTIC FOOTBALL CLUB 1888

	HEIGHT	WEIGHT	Date of Birth	Place of Birth		
	5ft 10ins	11st 11lbs	20/10/71	Sweden		
CAREER:	**SEASON**	**CLUB**	**APP.**	**GOALS**	**INTERNATIONAL CAPS**	
	93-97	Feyenoord	101	26	**APP.**	**GOALS**
	97-99	Celtic	70	44	34	7
					FORWARD	
					SQUAD NUMBER: 7	

PLAYER PROFILE
WIM JANSEN did much for Celtic as he ended Rangers' quest for 10-in-a-row before his bombshell decision to quit. But his masterstroke remains the capture of this lethal front man from Feyenoord for just £650,000. Quite simply the season of his life and a deserved double Player of the Year.

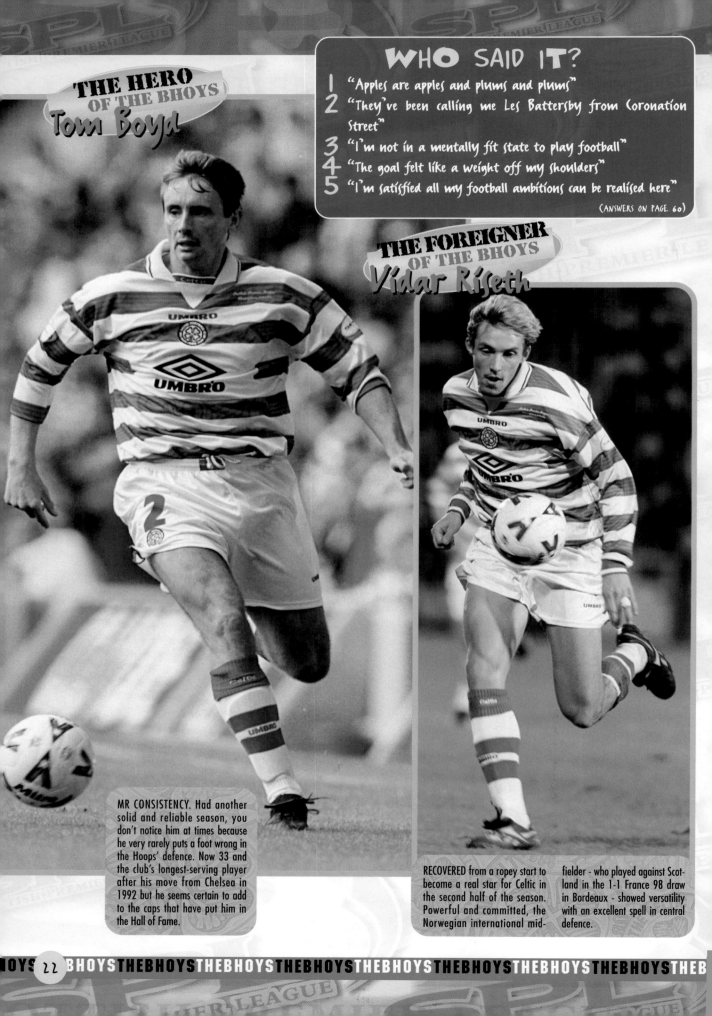

THE HERO
OF THE BHOYS
Tom Boyd

WHO SAID IT?

1 "Apples are apples and plums and plums"
2 "They've been calling me Les Battersby from Coronation Street"
3 "I'm not in a mentally fit state to play football"
4 "The goal felt like a weight off my shoulders"
5 "I'm satisfied all my football ambitions can be realised here"

(ANSWERS ON PAGE 60)

THE FOREIGNER
OF THE BHOYS
Vidar Riseth

MR CONSISTENCY. Had another solid and reliable season, you don't notice him at times because he very rarely puts a foot wrong in the Hoops' defence. Now 33 and the club's longest-serving player after his move from Chelsea in 1992 but he seems certain to add to the caps that have put him in the Hall of Fame.

RECOVERED from a ropey start to become a real star for Celtic in the second half of the season. Powerful and committed, the Norwegian international mid- fielder - who played against Scot- land in the 1-1 France 98 draw in Bordeaux - showed versatility with an excellent spell in central defence.

TWO MATCHES OF THE SEASON

November 21, 1998

CELTIC 5 RANGERS 1

SCOTT WILSON'S red card was the signal for merciless Celtic to embark on an exercise in humiliation led by Lubo Moravcik. The little Slovak scored twice and teenage terror Mark Burchill struck in the game's dying breath to avenge a Rangers win by the same score a decade earlier.

February 21, 1999

MOTHERWELL 1 CELTIC 7

THIS was the most astounding scoreline in a welter of Celtic thrashings for their stunned rivals. John Spencer was sent off early but Celtic - and Henrik Larsson - were set to run riot anyway and the slick Swede smacked home four in an unforgettable live Sky Sunday feast.

THE DISCOVERY OF THE BHOYS
Lubomír Moravčík

TOUGH to be called a 'find' when you are 33 years of age but it is true to say that little was known of this Slovakian wizard until Jozef Venglos bought his countryman for a bargain £300,000 from MSV Duisburg. Cunning and classy, his performance and two goals in the rout of Rangers will never be forgotten.

THE TRIVIA QUIZ

1 Who scored the goals that clinched 1998 title for Celtic in the 2-0 win over St Johnstone?
2 Who is Celtic's most capped player?
3 From which Italian side did Celtic sign Enrico Annoni?
4 Celtic beat Inter Milan to lift the European Cup in 1967 but who beat them in the Final three years later?
5 Which teams eliminated Celtic from Europe this season?

(ANSWERS ON PAGE 60)

DUNDEE

TEAM of the season in many ways for battling against all the odds on and off the pitch. The club was in dire financial straits when required to erect new stands to comply with SPL rules and, through an unsettled time, Jocky Scott managed to keep all his players focussed on the job of avoiding relegation. Scott is often painted as a grim character yet inside the game many players rate him their favourite coach and rave about him. His joy was complete when his side stayed up thanks to a 2-0 win at Dundee United. And he said: "Everyone tipped us to go down and no-one gave us a hope. They were wrong. The spirit of my players was always there and in the end we showed people something they perhaps didn't expect. We can play a bit too."

1893

THE HITMAN OF THE DEES
James Grady

HONOURS LIST

LEAGUE CHAMPIONSHIP (1)
DIVISION 1 1961-62; RUNNERS-UP: DIVISION 1 1902-03,
1906-07, 1908-09, 1948-49, 1980-81, 97-98.

SCOTTISH CUP (1)
1910; RUNNERS-UP: 1925, 1952, 1964.

LEAGUE CUP (3)
1951-52, 1952-53, 1973-74; RUNNERS-UP: 1967-68,
1980-81, (COCA COLA CUP): 1995-96.

B&Q (CENTENARY) CUP (1)
1990-91.
RUNNERS-UP: 1994-95.

MY HIGH FIVE

FAVOURITE BAND: U2
BEST MOVIE: In the name of the Father - Daniel Day Lewis.
OTHER TEAM: Celtic. I have a picture of Rangers' fanatic
Davie Cooper strangling me during our Clydebank days
which I treasure!
PIN-UP: Jennifer Aniston from Friends.
HOBBY AWAY FROM FOOTBALL: Squash - it started when I
worked in a sports centre.

PLAYER LIST

name	season 98-99 app	sub	goals	name	season 98-99 app	sub	goals
Robert Douglas	35			John Elliot	0		
Barry Smith	29	+4		Steve Milne	0		
Dave Rogers	7	+4		Lee Wilkie	0		
Dariusz Adamczuk	25	+1	6	Steven Boyack	7	+1	2
Brian Irvine	33		3	Gordon Hunter (to Nov. 98)	0		
Robbie Raeside	19	+2		Steven Tweed (from Dec. 98)	10	+1	1
Iain Anderson	17	+11	2	Jamie Langfield	1	+1	
Darren Magee	1	+1					
Eddie Annand	19	+10	9				
James Grady	20	+7	3				
Jim McInally	14	+1					
Derek Souter	0						
Craig Tully	0						
Lee Maddison	21						
Brian Grant	0	+4					
Willie Falconer	31	+2	4				
Stephane Pounewatchy	2	+1					
Gavin Strachan (to 20/12/98)	0	+1					
Lee Sharp (from 21/1/99)	4	+2					
Tommy Coyne	7	+9					
Shaun McSkimming	24	+4	2				
Willie Miller	28						
Eric Garcin	2	+1					
Derek Fleming	1						
Gavin Rae	23	+7	1				
Jerry O'Driscoll	0	+1					
Hugh Robertson	9	+1					
Michael Dickie	0						
Mark Slater	0						
Graham Bayne	0	+2					

HOME GROUND

DENS PARK
SANDEMAN STREET,
Dundee, DD3 7JY
Tel. (01382) 826104

CAPACITY
13,565 (seated 10,565 -
standing 3,000)

Pitch Dimensions
110 YDS X 72 YDS

THE MANAGER

Jocky Scott

PULLED off one of the achievements of his managerial life to hoist Dundee to fifth in a thrilling finish. The bargain basement £25,000 signing of midfielder Steven Boyack from Rangers was a masterstroke.

TEAM LINE-UP

Defence

Midfield

Attack

HOME
AND
AWAY

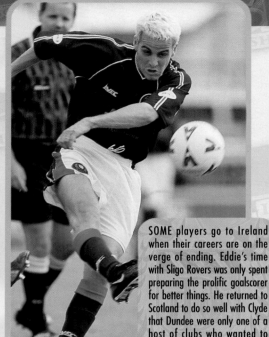

Season	Division	Pts	Final Pos.
1989/90	1	24	10
1990/91	1	52	3
1991/92	1	58	1
1992/93	P	34	10
1993/94	P	29	12
1994/95	1	68	3
1995/96	1	57	5
1996/97	1	58	3
1997/98	1	70	1
1998/99	P	46	5

10-YEAR RECORD

THE HERO
OF THE DEES
Eddie Annand

SOME players go to Ireland when their careers are on the verge of ending. Eddie's time with Sligo Rovers was only spent preparing the prolific goalscorer for better things. He returned to Scotland to do so well with Clyde that Dundee were only one of a host of clubs who wanted to bring him into Premier League. Helped Dundee to battle the odds and stay in the Major League after winning promotion.

Willie Miller

WILLIE was a fixture in Hibs' team for nine years before he left for Dens Park to show the same degree of dependability in a dark blue Jersey. There are no frills about his defensive play. But every team needs a determined force who understands that his priority is to keep his area of the park safe and leave the creative work to others.

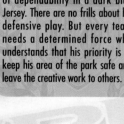

THE DISCOVERY
OF THE DEES
Iain Anderson

CONFIRMED in the SPL what he had shown in the First Division promotion campaign - he has star quality on the wing. Sadly, it came in what always looked his last season for the club before moving but he was a big hit and terrorised Rangers, scoring in a 1-1 April draw when the champions had the title jitters.

PLAYER PROFILE

FORMER brickie who has built himself a solid future at the very top after laying the foundations at first senior club Livingston. A commanding figure in the box coming for crossballs and his stature has grown since he was elevated to the Scotland squad and began to learn under the expert guidance of goalies' guru Alan Hodgkinson.

HEIGHT	WEIGHT	Date of Birth	Place of Birth
6ft 3ins	14st 12lbs	24/4/72	Lanark

CAREER:	SEASON	CLUB	APP.	GOALS
	93-95	Meadowbank Thistle	12	0
	95-97	Livingston	60	0
	97-99	Dundee	71	0

INTERNATIONAL CAPS	
APP.	GOALS

GOALKEEPER

SQUAD NUMBER: 1

DUNDEE UTD

DUNDEE UNITED FOOTBALL CLUB [1909]

DUNDEE UNITED cheated relegation but could not dodge the inevitable verdict that they are a team who are nowhere near realising their potential. Too many managers have now found that the shadow of former boss Jim McLean's achievements enveloped them. The bitter irony was that this season's victim was his brother Tommy and that the now United chairman Jim had to oversee his departure. Paul Sturrock, a goalscoring legend at the club during his playing days, was given the thorny job of restoring former glories to a side who reached the UEFA Cup Final 12 years ago. He did make one masterful signing to land Billy Dodds from Aberdeen in a package for Robbie Winters that also saw £700,000 flow into the coffers. But it's clear that this coming season will be one of major change at United and Sturrock said: "I've seen troubles at many clubs and the board are blamed. I realise the fans' frustration but surely they should look further down the pecking order at the players."

HONOURS LIST

LEAGUE CHAMPIONSHIP (1)
PREMIER DIVISION 1982-83.

SCOTTISH CUP (1)
1994; RUNNERS-UP: 1974, 1981, 1985, 1987, 1988, 1991.

LEAGUE CUP (2)
1979-80, 1980-81;
RUNNERS-UP: 1981-82, 1984-85, 1997-98.

EUROPEAN CUP
1983-84 (SEMI-FINALS)

UEFA CUP
RUNNERS-UP: 1986-87.

THE HITMAN OF THE ARABS
Joe Miller

MY HIGH FIVE

FAVOURITE BAND: U2

BEST MOVIE: The Godfather - choose any one of the three parts!

OTHER TEAM: Celtic, I played for them and supported them as a kid.

PIN-UP: Caprice, lucky man Tony Adams.

HOBBY AWAY FROM FOOTBALL: Golf, like most players.

PLAYER LIST

name	season 98-99			name	season 98-99		
	app	sub	goals		app	sub	goals
Sieb Dijkstra	26	+1		David Worrell	3	+2	
Iain Jenkins	5	+1		Stevie Fallon	0		
Maurice Malpas	31			Paul Gallacher	0		
Siggi Johsson	12	+2	1	David Partridge	0	+1	
Darren Patterson	17	+2		Bernard Pascual	16		
Erik Pedersen	6			Brian McLaughlin (from March. 99)	1		
Kjell Olofsson	32	+2	8	Stephen McConalogue	0	+1	
Lars Zetterlund	20	+1	1				
Roger Boli (to August 98)	4		1				
Jamie Dolan	5	+1					
Craig Easton	28	+2	1				
Gary McSwegan (to Oct. 98)	5	+1					
Alan Combe	10						
Robbie Winters (to Sept. 98)	1	+1					
Billy Dodds (from Sept. 98)	30	+1	16				
Joe Miller	14	+10	2				
Mark McNally	4	+1					
Andy McLaren	3	+6					
Neil Duffy	12		3				
Steve Thompson	5	+10	1				
Magnus Skoldmark	22	+3					
Jason de Vos	23	+2					
Tonny Mols	11						
Jose Valeriani	0	+1					
Neil Murray	4	+2					
John Eustace	8	+2	1				
Goran Marklund	0						
Scott McCulloch	9						
Dale Gray	0						
Jim Paterson	0	+7					

HOME GROUND

TANNADICE	TANNADICE STREET, Dundee, DD3 7JW. Tel. (01382) 833166
CAPACITY	14,209 (ALL SEATED)
Pitch Dimensions	110 YDS X 72 YDS.

THE MANAGER

Paul Sturrock

MOVED from the stable environment of St Johnstone to a daunting task trying to rediscover the glories of a club he helped make great as a player. Flirted with relegation for so long and Sturrock now knows the depth of the task ahead at a club that badly needs stability.

TEAM LINE-UP

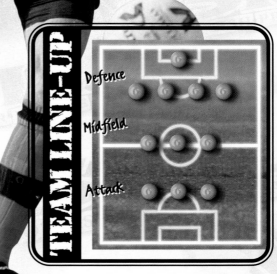

Defence

Midfield

Attack

HOME
AND
AWAY

Season	Division	Pts	Final Pos.
1989/90	P	35	4
1990/91	P	41	4
1991/92	P	51	4
1992/93	P	47	4
1993/94	P	42	6
1994/95	P	36	10
1995/96	1	67	2
1996/97	P	60	3
1997/98	P	37	7
1998/99	P	34	9

10-YEAR RECORD

THE HERO
OF THE ARABS
Maurice Malpas

SCOTLAND Hall of Fame member who will celebrate his 37th birthday at the dawn of the new season but is still going strong. Malpas has been at the core of United's defence for two decades now but the Tannadice side still depend so much on the player who doubles up as a coach these days.

THE DISCOVERY
OF THE ARABS
Craig Easton

STILL just 20 but Easton continues to develop into an excellent modern-day midfielder. Raised through the ranks, he has survived some difficult times with United and now his strong-running and passing skills look set to make him a major star of the future.

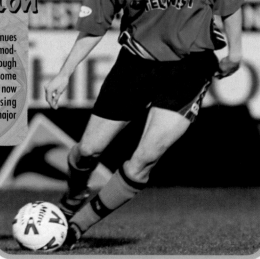

Iain Jenkins

ONE of the unluckiest players in football today. A car crash cost him months out of the game but he fought back to win a transfer from Chester to Tannadice last year. Then a serious back injury required surgery and meant that before the start of this season Iain had managed only twelve games in twelve months for his new club. If luck really balances itself out then Iain is due spectacular success in the future.

THE BEST
OF THE ARABS
Billy Dodds

DUNDEE UNITED
FOOTBALL CLUB

PLAYER PROFILE
SCOTLAND striker Doddsy has been the beating heart of Tannadice this season after his shock transfer took Robbie Winters the other way to Aberdeen. Gets better as he gets older and he reflected: "This may have been a disappointing season for United but it has without question been my best."

HEIGHT	WEIGHT	Date of Birth	Place of Birth
5ft 8ins	12st 2lbs	5/2/69	New Cumnock

SEASON	CLUB	APP.	GOALS
86-87	Chelsea	1	0
87-88	Partick T. (L)	30	9
88-89	Chelsea	2	0
89-93	Dundee	174	69
93-94	St Johnstone	20	6
94-98	Aberdeen	131	47
98-99	Dundee UTD	30	16

CAREER:

INTERNATIONAL CAPS

APP.	GOALS
9	3

FORWARD

SQUAD NUMBER: 14

THEARABS THEARABS THEARABS THEARABS THEARABS THEARABS THEARABS THEAR

HEARTS

HEARTS began the season as many experts' title dark horses and ended it struggling to stay out of the knacker's yard. The club's Tennents Scottish Cup Final win over Rangers had seemed the dawn of a new era at Tynecastle but after an opening day win over the eventual champs it all turned sour. The reasons? From the loss of Neil McCann to Gers and David Weir to Everton to the long-term injury to the hugely influential Colin Cameron. They are all solid explanations but they don't justify an alarming slump. New signings Steven Pressley, Gary McSwegan and Rab McKinnon didn't make the expected impact as the Jambos toiled at home on an awful pitch that needs major surgery this summer. Yet boss Jim Jefferies insisted: "There's no reason why we shouldn't be challenging at the right end of the table next time. I could go on forever about the reasons for our form lapse. But the simple truth is we lost key players through injury and transfers and the new lads took time to adjust."

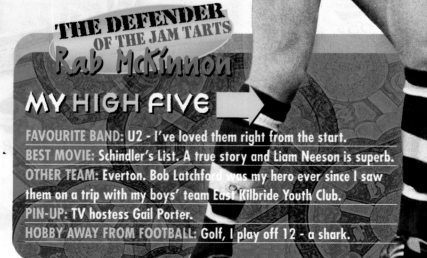

THE DEFENDER
OF THE JAM TARTS
Rab McKinnon

MY HIGH FIVE

FAVOURITE BAND: U2 - I've loved them right from the start.
BEST MOVIE: Schindler's List. A true story and Liam Neeson is superb.
OTHER TEAM: Everton. Bob Latchford was my hero ever since I saw them on a trip with my boys' team East Kilbride Youth Club.
PIN-UP: TV hostess Gail Porter.
HOBBY AWAY FROM FOOTBALL: Golf, I play off 12 - a shark.

HONOURS LIST

LEAGUE CHAMPIONSHIP (4)
DIVISION 1 1894-95, 1896-97, 1957-58, 1959-60;
RUNNERS-UP: DIVISION 1
1896-94, 1898-99, 1903-04, 1905-06, 1914-15,
1937-38, 1953-54, 1956-57, 1958-59, 1864-65;
PREMIER DIVISION 1985-86, 1987-88, 1991-92.

SCOTTISH CUP (6)
1891, 1896, 1901, 1906, 1956, 1998.

LEAGUE CUP (4)
1954-55, 1958-59, 1959-60, 1962-63

PLAYER LIST

name	season 98-99 app	sub	goals	name	season 98-99 app	sub	goals
Gilles Rousset	26			Robbie Nelson	0		
David McPherson	17	+1		Kris O'Neil	0	+3	
Gary Naysmith	23	+3		Vincent Guerin	9	+10	1
David Weir	22		1	Scott Strang	0		
Stefano Salvatori	11	+1		Juanjo Carricondo	1	+10	
Paul Ritchie	29		1	Gary Mc Swegan	17	+3	8
Neil McCann (to Jan. 99)	8		4				
Leigh Jenkinson (from Jan. 99)	3						
Steve Fulton	27		2				
Stephane Adam	28	+1	9				
Colin Cameron	10	+1	6				
Jim Hamilton (to Mar. 99)	20	+5	10				
Darren Jackson (from Apr. 99)	9		1				
Gary Locke	22	+3	1				
Roddie McKenzie	10						
Thomas Flogel	18	+2	2				
Jose Quitongo	4	+7					
Lee Makel	6	+7	1				
Rab McKinnon	14	+2					
Steven Pressley	29	+1	1				
Mohamed Berthe	1						
Stuart Callaghan	2						
Grant Murray	18	+5					
David Murie (Sep. to Oct. 98)	3						
Kevin James (from Apr. 99)	1	+3					
Myles Hogarth	0						
Derek Lilley (Dec. 98 to Jan. 99)	3	+1	1				
Andy Kirk (from Feb. 99)	0	+5					
Robert Horn	0						
Derek Holmes	1	+5					
Scott Severin	5	+2					
Kenny Milne	0						

HOME GROUND

TYNECASTLE

GORGIE ROAD,
Edinburgh, EH11 2NL
Tel. 0131-200 7200

CAPACITY

18,000 (ALL SEATED)

Pitch Dimensions

107 YDS X 74 YDS

Ticket Office

0131-200 7201

Credit card bookings

0131-200 7209

THE MANAGER

Jim Jefferies

AFTER all the plaudits of last season this has been a grim campaign for Jeff. But he showed the true character of a boss who reacts to trouble with the deadline day signing of Darren Jackson which proved instrumental in beating the drop.

TEAM LINE-UP

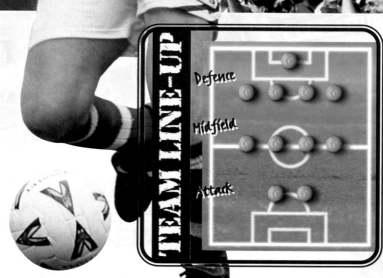

Defence
Midfield
Attack

HOME ⬆️
AND
AWAY ⬇️

10-YEAR RECORD

Season	Division	Pts	Final Pos.
1989/90	P	44	3
1990/91	P	35	5
1991/92	P	63	2
1992/93	P	44	5
1993/94	P	42	7
1994/95	P	43	6
1995/96	P	55	4
1996/97	P	52	4
1997/98	P	67	3
1998/99	P	42	6

THE HERO
OF THE JAM TARTS
Darren Jackson

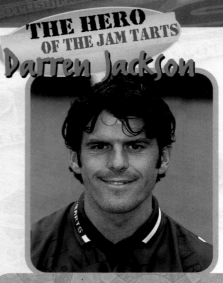

DEADLINE day signing from Celtic in March who knew he was on an all or nothing mission - after all, he had been a hero at HIBS! Jackson, the star who has recovered from brain surgery to keep his career on track, proved inspirational in keeping Hearts up but he smiled: "I knew that if things didn't work out I was going to be the bad guy."

THE FOREIGNER
OF THE JAM TARTS
Stephane Adam

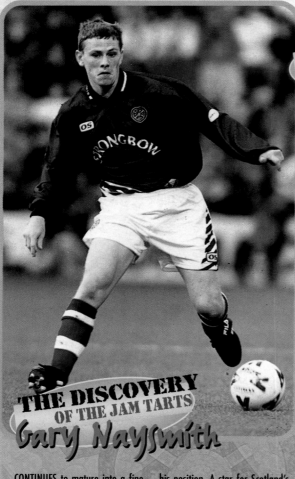

THE DISCOVERY
OF THE JAM TARTS
Gary Naysmith

CONTINUES to mature into a fine prospect at left-back and in the main he held off the powerful challenge of former FC Twente Enschede star Rab McKinnon for his position. A star for Scotland's under-21 side too and a player that babes' boss Alex Smith believes will mature into an international of the future.

LOOKED destined to depart the club this season and take the intelligent running and clever skills that have meant so much to the Jambos to either Rangers or Kilmarnock. But Jefferies' powers of persuasion worked and now the Frenchman from Metz has pledged himself to Tynecastle for another three years.

THE BEST
OF THE JAM TARTS
Steve Fulton

PLAYER PROFILE

LIFE is never simple for Steve. He was tipped for greatness at Celtic but failed to make the grade and left for English football. A return to the full Scotland squad after he had signed for Hearts seemed to signal a career that had been re-born. But last season was a disappointment on an individual level for a player who was caught up in Hearts' general decline. He'll be looking for better this time.

HEIGHT	WEIGHT	Date of Birth	Place of Birth
5ft 10ins	11st	10/8/70	Greenock

CAREER:	SEASON	CLUB	APP.	GOALS
	86-93	Celtic	76	2
	93-94	Bolton W.	4	-
	94-95	Falkirk	28	3
	95-98	Hearts	62	5

INTERNATIONAL CAPS	
APP.	GOALS

MIDFIELDER

SQUAD NUMBER: 8

HIBERNIAN

HIBERNIAN
FOOTBALL CLUB (1875)

RECORD-BREAKING Hibs racked up the highest number of wins on the trot in their club's history then bettered the top points total EVER achieved by First Division champions. After the desolation of relegation the delight of a season when the crowds rolled up at Easter Road and little went wrong. They dwarfed all around them in the First Division and looked a class apart. Now the hard work really starts for a manager reared under the legendary Alex Ferguson at Aberdeen. Alex McLeish has so far snubbed all talk of a return to Pittodrie as boss and is ready for the task ahead. He said: "You look for mentors in life and Fergie is mine. I can pick up the phone an talk to him at Manchester United, it's invaluable. I'm my own man but who wouldn't ask for advice from someone like him? He had a fire inside him in Dons and this season has shown his belief and will to win remain frightening."

HONOURS LIST

LEAGUE CHAMPIONSHIP
Division I 1902-03, 1947-48, 1950-51, 1951-52.
First Division 1980-81. Division II 1893-94, 1894-95,
1932-33; Division I 1896-97, 1946-47, 1949-50, 1952-53,
1973-74, 1974-75, 1998-99.

SCOTTISH CUP
1887, 1902.

LEAGUE CUP WINNERS
1972-73, 1981-92

EUROPEAN CUP
1955-56 (semi-finals)

UEFA CUP
1960-61 (Fair Cup, semi-finals)

THE STRIKER
OF THE HIBEES
Paul Hartley

MY HIGH FIVE

FAVOURITE BAND: M People.

BEST MOVIE: Goodfellas, gangsters at their best.

OTHER TEAM: Chelsea, it started with Ruud Gullit because he was my hero.

PIN-UP: Yasmin Le Bon.

HOBBY AWAY FROM FOOTBALL: Snooker, I like to think I'm a bit handy.

PLAYER LIST

name	season 98-99 app	sub	goals
Olle Gottskalksson	36		
Michael Renwick	15	+1	
David Elliot	8		
Paul Holsgrove	9	+8	1
John Hughes	22	+1	3
Shaun Dennis	29	+2	3
Stuart Lovell	26	+3	11
Justin Skinner	24		2
Stevie Crawford	27	+7	14
Barry Lavely	9	+17	2
Pat McGinlay	29	+1	12
Tony Rougier	10	+5	1
Scott Bannerman	2	+9	
Eric Paton	1	+3	
Peter Guggi	7	+1	2
Kevin Harper	0	+2	1
Rab Shannon	1		
Paul Tosh	1		
Barry Prenderville	13		2
Mixu Paatelainen	25	+1	12
Derek Anderson	6		
Kenny Miller	5	+2	1
Russel Latapy	22		6
Paul Lovering	12		1
Derek Collins	16		
Mark Dempsey	5	+3	
Paul Hartley	6	+6	5
Tom Smith	3	+2	
Alex Marinkov	10		1
Franck Sauzee	9		2
Alan Reid	-	+1	
Emilio Bottiglieri	-	+1	
Tom McManus	-	+1	
Own goals			1

HOME GROUND

EASTER ROAD STADIUM

	Albion Rd,
	Edinburgh EH7 5QG.
Telephone	0131 661 2159.
Fax	0131 659 6488
CAPACITY	16,218 (ALL SEATED)
Pitch Dimensions	112 YDS X 74 YDS.
Ticket Office	(0131) 661 1875

THE MANAGER

Alex McLeish

ALL season long big Eck's Hibees carried the mantle of favourites for promotion and despite an early shock when they lost at home to Stranraer they lived up to it. Now he takes a team with a winning mentality back into the top flight after winning the championship by an amazing 23 points.

TEAM LINE-UP

Defence

Midfield

Attack

10-YEAR RECORD

Season	Division	Pts	Final Pos.
1989/90	P	34	7
1990/91	P	25	9
1991/92	P	49	5
1992/93	P	37	7
1993/94	P	47	5
1994/95	P	53	3
1995/96	P	43	5
1996/97	P	38	9
1997/98	P	30	10
1998/99	1	89	1

TOP SCORERS

	League	Cup	Europe	Total
Steve Crawford	14			14
Pat McGinlay	12			12
Mixu Paatelainen	12			12
Stewart Lovell	11			11
Russell Latapy	6	1		7

THE HERO
OF THE HIBEES
Mixu Paatalainen

HITMAN Mixu has been down south with Bolton and Wolves and his mix of brains and brawn returns to Scotland's top flight after his days at Aberdeen and Dundee United. The Finnish international is 32 now but has proven credentials in the SPL with 56 goals in 208 league games at Pittodrie and Tannadice.

THE FOREIGNER
OF THE HIBEES
Franck Sauzee

EUROPEAN CUP winner with Marseille who was easing through life at the back for Montpellier when McLeish swooped. The former French international - remembered in Scotland for his goal that denied Rangers a Champions League Final place in 1993 - has midfield pedigree that will be vital next season.

THE DISCOVERY
OF THE HIBEES
Olle Gottskalksson

THE towering Icelandic keeper - signed two years ago from Keflavik - seemed lost in the Easter Road shadows after his form dipped and ex-Scotland keeper Bryan Gunn arrived at the club. But when Gunn's career was ended by a serious injury Olle found courage in Hibs' hour of need to fight his way back this season.

Season 1998/99 Results - by Date

4/8	Morton 0, Hibs 1
15/8	Hibs 1, Stranraer 2
22/8	Falkirk 1, Hibs 1
29/8	Hibs 4, Ayr Utd. 2
5/9	Clydebank 2, Hibs 2
12/9	St. Mirren 2, Hibs 0
19/9	Hibs 3, Raith Rovers 1
26/9	Hibs 0, Hamilton Ac. 0
3/10	Airdrieonians 1, Hibs 3
10/10	Stranraer 0, Hibs 1
17/10	Hibs 2, Morton 1
24/10	Ayr Utd. 3, Hibs 3
31/10	Hibs 2, Clydebank 1,
7/11	Raith Rovers 1, Hibs 3
21/11	Hamilton Ac. 2, Hibs 2
24/11	Hibs 4, St. Mirren 1
28/11	Hibs 1, Airdrieonians 0
5/12	Morton 1, Hibs 3
12/12	Hibs 2, Falkirk 1
19/12	Hibs 3, Clydebank 0
26/12	Hibs 3, Ayr Utd. 0
2/1	Hibs 5, Raith Rovers 1
9/1	St. Mirren 1, Hibs 2
16/1	Hibs 4, Hamilton Ac. 0
30/1	Airdrieonians 0, Hibs 4
6/2	Hibs 2, Stranraer 0
20/2	Falkirk 1, Hibs 2
27/2	Ayr Utd. 1, Hibs 3
14/3	Clydebank 2, Hibs 0
20/3	Hibs 3, Airdrieonians 0
3/4	Hamilton Ac. 0, Hibs 2
10/4	Raith Rovers 1, Hibs 3
17/4	Hibs 2, St. Mirren 1
24/4	Hibs 2, Morton 1
1/5	Stranraer 0, Hibs 4
8/5	Hibs 2, Falkirk 1

THE BEST OF THE HIBEES
Russel Latapy

PLAYER PROFILE

MANCHESTER UNITED superstar Dwight Yorke's best buddy but this brilliant midfielder is making his own headlines now. The Trinidad and Tobago star was a shrewd McLeish signing just when Hibs needed him most and he was voted First Division Player of the Year by his fellow professionals to confirm his quality.

HEIGHT	WEIGHT	Date of Birth	Place of Birth
5ft 7ins	11st	2/8/68	Trinidad

SEASON	CLUB	APP.	GOALS
94-96	FC Porto (P)	40	6
96-98	Boavista (P)	40	1
from Oct. 98-99	Hibernian	22	6

INTERNATIONAL CAPS	
APP.	GOALS

MIDFIELDER

SQUAD NUMBER:

HIBEES HIBEES HIBEES HIBEES HIBEES HIBEES HIBEES HIBEES HIBEES HIBEES HIBEES HIBEES HIBEES HI

KILMARNOCK

KILMARNOCK FOOTBALL CLUB (1869)

BOBBY WILLIAMSON is fast growing into a young manager of high repute as his shrewd football mind ticks over. Took criticism when he shelled out big wages to attract ThirtySomething Ibrox idols Ian Durrant and Ally McCoist to the club in the summer. The signings, though, were a masterstroke. Durrant, who had languished too long in the Rangers reserves, responded with one of the seasons of his life as almost every Killie move was channelled through their rejuvenated playmaker. McCoist was plagued by injury but scored a memorable hat-trick against Hearts and raised the club's PR profile beyond recognition. Killie's success was built on the solid bedrock of a brilliant defence and behind them outstanding keeper Gordon Marshall equalled the club's shut-out record. Williamson revealed: "We worked all season dedicating one day a week to an intensive session on defence because I feel all good sides build from the back. It paid off."

THE HITMAN OF KILLIE
Ally McCoist

MY HIGH FIVE

FAVOURITE BAND: The Clash - Punk dragged me through the best years of my life.

BEST MOVIE: One Flew over the Cuckoo's Nest although Jim Carrey was brilliant playing me in Liar, Liar!

FAVOURITE OTHER TEAM: Rangers - and that's a silly question.

PIN-UP: Cindy Crawford, I like my girls to be women.

HOBBY AWAY FROM FOOTBALL: Music, I play the bass guitar badly but no-one looks better posing in front of the mirror.

HONOURS LIST

LEAGUE CHAMPIONSHIP (1)
DIVISION 1 1964-65;
RUNNERS-UP:
DIVISION 1 1959-60, 1960-61, 1962-63, 1963-64.

SCOTTISH CUP (3)
1920, 1929, 1997;
RUNNERS-UP:
1898, 1932, 1938, 1957, 1960.

LEAGUE CUP
RUNNERS-UP: 1952-53,
1960-61, 1962-63.

PLAYER LIST

name	season 98-99 app	sub	goals
Gordon Marshall	36		
Gus McPherson	31		1
Dylan Kerr	16		
Ray Montgomerie	22		
Kevin McGowne	32		4
John Henry	7	+4	3
Pat Nevin (to Oct. 98)	2	+1	1
Mark Reilly (from Oct. 98)	17	+1	
Gary Holt	33		3
Paul Wright	25	+8	6
Ian Durrant	36		4
Ally Mitchell	27	+6	4
Colin Meldrum	0		
Ally McCoist	16	+10	7
Alan Mahood	16	+12	2
Jerome Vareille	20	+3	5
Martin Baker	23		
Steve Hamilton	5		
Martin O'Neill	0		
Mark Roberts	9	+13	3
Alan Kerr	0		
Chris Innes	4		1
Jim Lauchlan	14		
David Bagan	1	+4	
Gary Hay	0		
Alex Burke	2	+16	
Rod Lennox	0		
Gary McCutcheon	2	+10	2
Stuart Davidson	0		
Adam Strain	0		

HOME GROUND

RUGBY PARK

CAPACITY
Pitch Dimensions
Ticket Information

RUGBY ROAD,
Kilmarnock, KA1 2DP.
Tel. (01563) 525184
18,128 (ALL SEATED)
112 YDS X 74 YDS.
(0891) 633249

THE MANAGER

Bobby Williamson

CAPTURING Bobby Williamson on a five-year deal until 2003 was the best signing resurgent Kilmarnock have made. Despite being a striker as a player in his days with the likes of Rangers and Killie his biggest coaching triumph has been creating that mean machine defence at Rugby Park.

TEAM LINE-UP

Defence

Midfield

Attack

HOME ↑
AND
AWAY ↓

THE HERO
OF KILLIE
Kevin McGowne

Season	Division	Pts	Final Pos.
1989/90	2	48	2
1990/91	1	43	5
1991/92	1	54	4
1992/93	1	54	2
1993/94	P	40	8
1994/95	P	43	7
1995/96	P	41	7
1996/97	P	39	7
1997/98	P	50	4
1998/99	P	56	4

10-YEAR RECORD

WON a deserved four-year deal after a superb season at the back alongside veteran skipper Ray Montgomerie. Monty's departure means a new partnership with Jim Lauchlan but Kevin said: "I will never forget the debt I owe Ray, he's taught me so much."

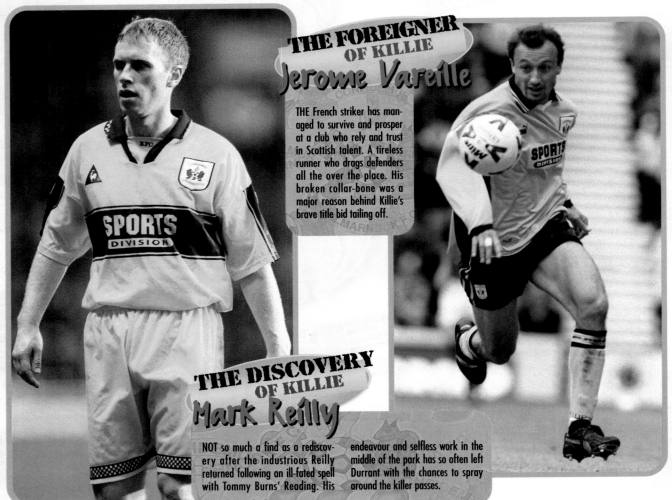

THE FOREIGNER
OF KILLIE
Jerome Vareille

THE French striker has managed to survive and prosper at a club who rely and trust in Scottish talent. A tireless runner who drags defenders all the over the place. His broken collar-bone was a major reason behind Killie's brave title bid tailing off.

THE DISCOVERY
OF KILLIE
Mark Reilly

NOT so much a find as a rediscovery after the industrious Reilly returned following an ill-fated spell with Tommy Burns' Reading. His endeavour and selfless work in the middle of the park has so often left Durrant with the chances to spray around the killer passes.

THE BEST
OF KILLIE
Ian Durrant

CONFIDEMUS
KILMARNOCK F.C.

SPORTS DIVISION

PLAYER PROFILE
REVITALISED by his move from Rangers, he had one of the seasons of his life at the age of 32. Love of the club kept him at Ibrox when he was a bit-part player but he's now back for Scotland and he confessed: "After the three years out through injury I just enjoy every game. I should have left Gers sooner."

HEIGHT	WEIGHT	Date of Birth	Place of Birth
5ft 8ins	9st 7lb	29/10/66	Glasgow

	SEASON	CLUB	APP.	GOALS
CAREER:	84-98	Rangers	249	26
	98-99	Kilmarnock	36	4

INTERNATIONAL CAPS

APP.	GOALS
16	0

MIDFIELDER
SQUAD NUMBER: 10

KILLIE KILLIE KILLIE KILLIE KILLIE KILLIE KILLIE KILLIE KILLIE KILLIE KILLIE KILLIE KILLIE KILLIE KILLIE KILLIE

MOTHERWELL

WELL'S experiment with Finnish coach Harri Kampman was short-lived and the appointment of rookie boss Billy Davies as his replacement was a shock. Davies then went through more in one season than many bosses might in five. He saw the club branded New Motherwell as - backed by enthusiastic club owner John Boyle - he made imaginative signings like Scotland striker John Spencer who just happens to be the manager's brother-in-law! Spenny, Ged Brannan and former Rangers keeper Andy Goram were instrumental in all things good from Well but the bad was just around the corner. Tragedy struck when youth team player Andy Thompson died aged just 19. Then Spencer was sent off in the 7-1 home mauling from Celtic. Davies confessed: "You could say I've had a crash-course in management but I'll learn from it. The main job this season was to stay up, now the real work begins."

HONOURS LIST

LEAGUE CHAMPIONSHIP (1)
DIVISION 1: 1931-32;
RUNNERS-UP: PREMIER DIVISION 1994-95.
DIVISION 1 1926-27, 1929-30, 1932-33, 1933-34.

SCOTTISH CUP (2)
1952, 1991.
RUNNERS-UP: 1931, 1933, 1939, 1951.

LEAGUE CUP (1)
1950-51; RUNNERS-UP:
1954-55.

THE STRIKER OF THE WELL
Lee McCulloch

MY HIGH FIVE ➔

FAVOURITE BAND: The Charlatans.
BEST MOVIE: Lock, Stock and Two Smoking Barrels - well played Vinnie Jones!!
OTHER TEAM: Arsenal.
PIN-UP: Danni or Kylie Minogue - I just can't make my mind up.
HOBBY AWAY FROM FOOTBALL: It has to be the typical footballer one of golf - I play off 12.

PLAYER LIST

name	season 98-99 app	sub	goals	name	season 98-99 app	sub	goals
Stevie Woods	7			Steve Reilly	0		
Eddie May	10	+2		Steve Hammell	0		
Steve McMillan	30		2	Herve Bacque	0	+1	
Jamie McGowan	32	1		Sandy Hodge	0		
Ged Brannan	25		5	David Docherty	0		
Greig Denham	0			Scott Crawford	0		
Ian Ross	8	+3		David Dunn	0		
Simo Valakari	35			Craig Callaghan	0		
Stephen Halliday	2	+2		Derek Adams	10	+13	3
Brian McClair (to Dec. 98)	8	+2		John Spencer	21		7
Mark Gower (from Mar. 99)	8	+1	1	Colin Miller	0		
Owen Coyle (to Mar. 99)	26			Kevin McLaughlin	0		
Steve Nicholas (from Apr. 99)	1	+6	1	Keith Lasley	0		
Jan Michels	7	+3		Don Goodman	8		1
Mikko Kaven	16						
Kevin Christie	4	+1					
Eliphas Shivute (to Aug. 98)	0	+1					
Tony Thomas (from Dec. 98)	10						
Billy Davies	0						
Mickey Weir	0						
Lee McCulloch	14	+12	3				
Michel Doesburg	30						
Rob Matthaei	14	+3					
Steven Craigan	6	+4					
Jered Stirling	4		1				
Douglas Ramsey	0	+4					
Greg Miller	1	+3					
Daniel Kemp	0						
David White	0						
Phil Bannister	0						
Shaun Teale	29		1				
Kai Nyyssonen (to Dec. 98)	0	+3	1				
Andy Goram (from Jan. 99)	13						
Pat Nevin	16	+15					

HOME GROUND

FIR PARK — 1-39 FIRPARK STREET, Motherwell, ML1 2QN. Tel. (01698) 333333

CAPACITY — 13,742 (ALL SEATED)

Pitch Dimensions — 110 YDS X 75 YDS.

TICKET OFFICE — (01698) 333030

THE MANAGER

Billy Davies

TOUGH season but if dedication brings success he'll make it. Davies has 20 years worth of books he has kept detailing almost every training session he has taken part in. Also used pal Paul Lambert's Borussia Dortmund experience to improve his knowledge.

TEAM LINE-UP

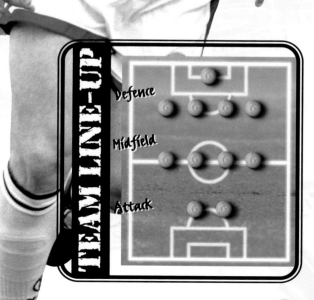

Defence

Midfield

Attack

HOME ↑
AND
↓ AWAY

Season	Division	Pts	Final Pos.
1989/90	P	34	6
1990/91	P	33	6
1991/92	P	34	10
1992/93	P	35	9
1993/94	P	56	3
1994/95	P	56	2
1995/96	P	39	8
1996/97	P	58	8
1997/98	P	34	9
1998/99	P	41	7

10-YEAR RECORD

HEARTBROKEN when Dick Advocaat decided he had to leave his beloved Rangers but the man they simply call The Goalie has battled back. His impact at his new club was summed up by one astonishing save from a Henrik Larsson header when he almost single-handedly pulled off a draw in April before the Swede's match-winning penalty.

THE HERO
OF THE WELL
Andy Goram

THE DISCOVERY
OF THE WELL
Ged Brannan

GIFTED playmaker whose career had gone awry at Manchester City before Davies swooped with a £378,000 transfer fee. Liverpool-born but he loves Scotland so much now he is investigating his family background to see if he can qualify to play for us at international level. A welcome addition to the SPL.

Jamie McGowan

THE central defender who was signed by Dundee from Morecambe for just £ 1,000 has blossomed into an outstanding player. He left Dens Park and helped Falkirk into the Scottish Cup final against Kilmarnock in 1997 before leaving there and going to Motherwell. Now married to a Scottish girl, the Liverpool born Jamie will be an important part of Billy Davies' plans at Fir Park.

MOTOROLA

PLAYER PROFILE
UNSUNG hero but every Well player belts out his praises when you ask them. Does all the spadework for more creative talents like Brannan and gets through a frightening amount of graft. The Finnish international midfielder has been an excellent import since switching to Scotland two years ago.

HEIGHT	WEIGHT	Date of Birth	Place of Birth
5ft 10ins	11st 11lbs	28/4/73	Helsinki, Finland

SEASON	CLUB	APP.	GOALS	INTERNATIONAL CAPS	
				APP.	GOALS
94-96	Finn PA	48	5		
96-99	Motherwell	74	0		

MIDFIELDER

SQUAD NUMBER: 8

RANGERS

RANGERS FOOTBALL CLUB (1873)

DICK ADVOCAAT had managed Holland and won a war of words with Ruud Gullit that ended the Dreadlocked One's international career. He'd taken PSV Eindhoven to the heights in his homeland and drawn admiring glances from European giants like Real Madrid. But when he needed a fresh challenge he chose a daunting task, he elected to take on the rebuilding of Rangers. One season - and £25million of chairman David Murray's money later he has put Gers back on top of the pile in Scotland and won the Treble. Regaining the title lost at the end of Walter Smith's glorious nine-in-a-row era was the prime target but the shrewd Advocaat has exceeded expectations and given the club some pride back in Europe too. Now after a UEFA Cup run to the last 16 before defeat from Parma he's desperate to build on that after agreeing a new deal to stay as boss until 2002. And he said: "I'm delighted to remain here longer because it will give me the chance to take Rangers to where I want them to be."

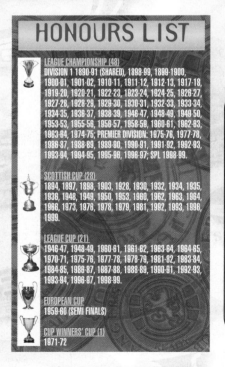

HONOURS LIST

LEAGUE CHAMPIONSHIP (48)
DIVISION 1 1890-91 (SHARED), 1898-99, 1899-1900, 1900-01, 1901-02, 1910-11, 1911-12, 1912-13, 1917-18, 1919-20, 1920-21, 1922-23, 1923-24, 1924-25, 1926-27, 1927-28, 1928-29, 1929-30, 1930-31, 1932-33, 1933-34, 1934-35, 1936-37, 1938-39, 1946-47, 1948-49, 1949-50, 1953-53, 1955-56, 1956-57, 1958-59, 1960-61, 1962-83, 1863-64, 1974-75; PREMIER DIVISION: 1975-76, 1977-78, 1986-87, 1988-89, 1989-90, 1990-91, 1991-92, 1992-93, 1993-94, 1994-95, 1995-96, 1996-97; SPL 1998-99.

SCOTTISH CUP (28)
1894, 1897, 1898, 1903, 1928, 1930, 1932, 1934, 1935, 1936, 1948, 1949, 1950, 1953, 1960, 1962, 1963, 1964, 1966, 1973, 1976, 1978, 1979, 1981, 1992, 1993, 1996, 1999.

LEAGUE CUP (21)
1946-47, 1948-49, 1960-61, 1961-62, 1963-64, 1964-65, 1970-71, 1975-76, 1977-78, 1978-79, 1981-82, 1983-84, 1984-85, 1986-87, 1987-88, 1988-89, 1990-91, 1992-93, 1993-94, 1996-97, 1998-99.

EUROPEAN CUP
1959-60 (SEMI FINALS)

CUP WINNERS' CUP (1)
1971-72

THE MANAGER

Dick Advocaat

THE man they call the Little General has survived some questionable buys like Stephane Guivarc'h to emerge with his reputation enhanced and silverware back in the Ibrox trophy cabinet. An inspirational choice to succeed Walter Smith.

MY HIGH FIVE

FAVOURITE BAND: Iron Maiden
BEST MOVIE: Midnight Express
OTHER TEAM: Juventus FC
PIN-UP: Barbara, my wife
HOBBY AWAY FROM FOOTBALL: My family and to play squash

THE STOPPER OF THE GERS
Sergio Porrini

PLAYER LIST

name	season 98-99 app	sub	goals	name	season 98-99 app	sub	goals
Lionel Charbonnier	11			Colin Hendry	15	+3	
Sergio Porrini	36		2	Robert Malcolm	0		
Lorenzo Amoruso	34		1	Allan McGregor	0		
Daniel Prodan	0			Lee Feeney	0	+1	
Arthur Numan	8	+2		Paul McKnight	0		
Barry Ferguson	22		1	Claudio Reyna	3		
Andrei Kanchelskis	31	+1	7				
Giovanni van Bronckhorst	36		7				
Gordon Durie	1	+4					
Gabriel Amato	14	+7	6				
Jorg Albertz	34	+1	11				
Jonas Thern	1						
Antii Niemi	7						
Ian Ferguson	4	+6					
Stephane Guivarc'h	12	+4	5				
Rod Wallace	34		19				
Derek McInnes	0	+8					
Gennaro Gattuso (to Oct. 98)	3	+3					
Neil McCann (from Jan. 99)	16	+3	5				
Craig Moore (to Oct.98)	8		1				
Stefan Klos (from Dec. 98)	19						
Jonatan Johansson	12	+13	8				
Stale Stensaas	1	+1					
Scott Wilson	8	+6	1				
David Graham	0	+3					
Barry Nicholson	3	+4					
Tony Vidmar	27	+3	1				
Theo Snelders	0						
Charlie Miller	2	+15	3				
Luigi Riccio	0	+1					
Sebastian Rozental	0	+3					
Darren Fitzgerald	0						

TEAM LINE-UP

Defence

Midfield

Attack

HOME GROUND

IBROX STADIUM	150 EDMISTON DRIVE GLASGOW, G51 2XD TEL. (0141) 427 8500
CAPACITY	50,411 (ALL SEATED)
Pitch Dimensions	115 YDS X 75 YDS
Ticket Office	TEL (0141) 427 8800 FAX (0141) 427 8504

HOME
AND
AWAY

10-YEAR RECORD

Season	Division	Pts	Final Pos.
1989/90	P	51	1
1990/91	P	55	1
1991/92	P	72	1
1992/93	P	73	1
1993/94	P	58	1
1994/95	P	69	1
1995/96	P	87	1
1996/97	P	80	1
1997/98	P	72	2
1998/99	P	77	1

WHEN THE GOALS WERE SCORED

	0-15	16-30	31-45	46-60	61-75	79-90
Rangers	11	11	10	16	10	20

	League	Cup	Europe	Total
Rod Wallace	19	5	3	27
Jorg Albertz	11	4	4	19
Jonatan Johansson	8	4	5	17
Neil McCann	8	3	1	12 *
Giovanni Van Bronckhorst	7	1	2	10

* 4 for Hearts

TRUE OR FALSE?

1. Rangers were formed in 1872, true or false?
2. When the club beat Moscow Dynamo 3-2 in the Final of the European Cup Winners' Cup in 1972 the scorers were Willie Johnston (2) and Colin Stein, true or false?
3. When Celtic won the European Cup in 1967 Gers lost a Cup Winners' Cup Final to Nuremburg, true or false?
4. Rangers legend Tom Forsyth was famously christened Jaws, true or false?
5. Chris Woods was Graeme Souness' first signing for Rangers, true or false?

(ANSWERS ON PAGE 61)

THE BEST
OF THE GERS
Giovanni Van Bronckhorst

RANGERS FOOTBALL CLUB
READY

PLAYER PROFILE

JOEY as he's known inside the walls of Ibrox has been an instant hit in the Rangers' midfield thanks to his refusal to bask in his £5million transfer fee and his constant willingness to graft for the team. The combative playmaker's passion and commitment match his poise and class in possession.

HEIGHT	WEIGHT	Date of Birth	Place of Birth
5ft 10ins	11st14lbs	5/2/75	Rotterdam, Netherlands

CAREER:	SEASON	CLUB	APP.	GOALS	INTERNATIONAL CAPS	
					APP.	GOALS
	97-99	From Feyenoord Rangers	72	14	7	1

MIDFIELDER

SQUAD NUMBER: 8

THE HERO
OF THE GERS
Rod Wallace

NICKED from Leeds United for free on the Bosman ruling and has proved a marvellous signing. Gave defenders massive headaches all season as he dropped off the front to find space and then darted forward into the danger zone. Clever player who has adapted to a string of different partners up front.

WHO SAID IT?

1 "He's done not bad for a beginner"

2 "Gravedigging wasn't one of my better jobs"

3 "It wasn't my fault, the ball hit a frosty patch"

4 "It's my first hat-trick for Rangers but I look like leaving, it's terrible"

5 "When I heard that song I thought I'd cry"

(ANSWERS ON PAGE 61)

THE DISCOVERY
OF THE GERS
Barry Ferguson

BARRY was on his way out until Advocaat arrived and built a team around the gifted 21-year-old playmaker. One classic turn and pass in the UEFA Cup win in Leverkusen sums up why the Dutchman was spot on. Has the ability to succeed where brother Derek failed and become THE player of his generation.

THE GAMES THAT MATTERED

December 26, 1998
Rangers 1 St Johnstone 0
COLIN HENDRY'S handball on the line meant a red card but Saints' John O'Neil blazed the penalty off the bar. A gritty fightback was capped by Sergio Porrini's winner and three vital points.

May 2,1999
Celtic 0 Rangers 3
THE biggest Old Firm game for 20 years and the day Neil McCann was born as a True Blue hero. He scored twice in an explosive match as Gers clinched the title on the turf of their bitterest foes.

THE TRIVIA QUIZ

1 Where was Finnish international striker Jonatan Johannson born?

2 Who was named the Greatest Ever Ranger during the season after a fans' poll?

3 From which club did Rangers sign injury-plagued defender Daniel Prodan?

4 Rangers' Dutch left-back Arthur Numan landed a France 98 red card against which nation?

5 Who wore No.40 in the Rangers' squad this season?

(ANSWERS ON PAGE 61)

THE FOREIGNER OF THE GERS
Lorenzo Amoruso

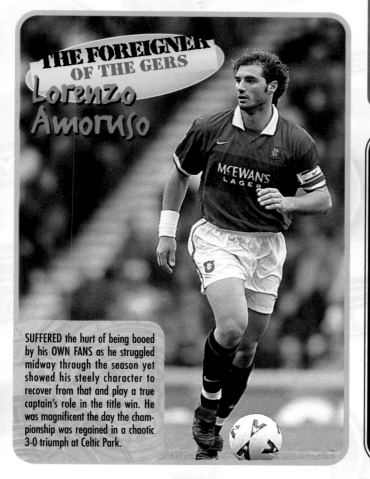

SUFFERED the hurt of being booed by his OWN FANS as he struggled midway through the season yet showed his steely character to recover from that and play a true captain's role in the title win. He was magnificent the day the championship was regained in a chaotic 3-0 triumph at Celtic Park.

ARE YOU EAGLE-EYED?

CAN you spot the scrambled Rangers star in action here and the rival he is clashing with?

ST. JOHNSTONE

ST. JOHNSTONE FOOTBALL CLUB [1884]

LEAGUE CUP runners-up, Scottish Cup semi-finalists, third in the league and qualified for Europe. That is the sum total of what adds up to the season of Sandy Clark's managerial life. So cruelly jettisoned by Hearts when he had raised a generation of class kids, Clark recovered at Hamilton Accies before taking the Saints job when Paul Sturrock quit for Dundee United. Now the former Rangers and West Ham striker has brought the grit and guile he had as a player to management at the top level. He confessed: "What happened at Hearts hurt a lot at the time and while it's hard to forgive you don't dwell on it and torment yourself. You have the option of sitting and feeling sorry for yourself but instead I picked myself up and got on again. Now a superb squad effort has done this for Saints, I'm looking forward to the UEFA Cup."

THE MIDFIELDER OF THE SAINTS
Paul Kane

MY HIGH FIVE →

FAVOURITE BAND: The Proclaimers - I loved Sunshine on Leith when it came out and still do.

BEST MOVIE: Silence of the Lambs, thrill a minute.

OTHER TEAM: Hibs, I'm looking forward to tangling with my first club again this season.

PIN-UP: My daughter Natasha who is two and adorable.

HOBBY AWAY FROM FOOTBALL:
Golf, I play during the summer.

PLAYER LIST

name	season 98-99 app	sub	goals
Alan Main	34		
John McQuillan	27	+1	1
Allan Preston	8	+1	1
Nick Dasovic	31		1
Jim Weir	6		1
Alan Kernaghan	26		3
Phil Scott	14	+2	2
John O'Neil	32		2
Robby Grant	14	+12	4
George O'Boyle	12	+1	2
Paul Kane	33	+1	3
Gerry McMahon	13	+7	1
Paddy Connolly	7	+2	1
Garry Bollan	32		4
Danny Griffin	14	+5	1
Keith O'Halloran	9	+6	
Steve Robertson	0		
Stuart McCluskey	5	+2	
John Paul McBride	2	+1	
Andy Whiteford	0	+1	
Allan Ferguson	2	+1	
Keiran McAnespie	9	+9	2
Darren Dods	34		2
Stuart Malcolm	0		
Marc McCulloch	0		
Nathan Lowndes	12	+18	2
Miguel Simao	20	+7	4
Keigan Parker	0	+2	

HOME GROUND

Mc DIARMID PARK	CRIEFF ROAD, Perth, PH1 2SJ. Tel. (01738) 459090
CAPACITY	10,673 (ALL SEATED)
Pitch Dimensions	115 YDS X 75 YDS.
TICKET OFFICE	(01738) 459090

THE MANAGER

Sandy Clark

CAN be justifiably proud of a remarkable season and of a remarkable statistic from his third-placed side. Starved of a top-notch striker, all 19, of his regular outfield first team squad scored this season!

TEAM LINE-UP

Defence

Midfield

Attack

HOME
AND
AWAY

Season	Division	Pts	Final Pos.
1989/90	1	58	1
1990/91	P	31	7
1991/92	P	36	8
1992/93	P	40	6
1993/94	P	40	10
1994/95	1	56	5
1995/96	1	65	4
1996/97	1	80	1
1997/98	P	48	5
1998/99	P	57	3

10-YEAR RECORD

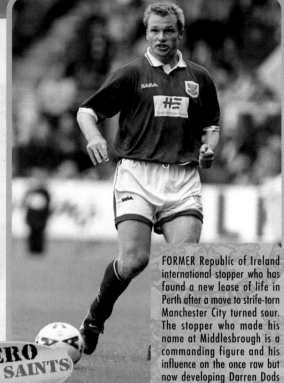

THE HERO OF THE SAINTS
Alan Kernaghan

FORMER Republic of Ireland international stopper who has found a new lease of life in Perth after a move to strife-torn Manchester City turned sour. The stopper who made his name at Middlesbrough is a commanding figure and his influence on the once raw but now developing Darren Dods has been massive.

THE FOREIGNER OF THE SAINTS
Nick Dasovic

ONE of Scottish football's larger than life characters, the former guitarist in a rock band is now a feared competitor in the SPL midfield battle zone. Capped 34 times for Canada yet reared as a player in his parents' homeland of Croatia where he was with Dinamo Zagreb.

THE DISCOVERY OF THE SAINTS
Miguel Simao

PLUNDERING Europe can be a treacherous transfer business but Sandy Clark inherited gold with this elusive Portuguese forward. Perfectly suited to the Saints' counter-attacking system, he has a brilliant left foot and pace to burn that has troubled every defence he has faced this season.

THE BEST
OF THE SAINTS
John O'Neil

ST. JOHNSTONE F.C.

XARA

hₑ
Scottish Hydro-Electric

Mitre

PLAYER PROFILE
ONE of the first names down in any pundit's squad of the season and that's a huge compliment at an unfashionable club such as Saints. This invaluable midfielder developed in the Jim McLean school at Tannadice is now at his peak. His deft use of the ball has surely put him on the fringe of Scotland honours.

HEIGHT	WEIGHT	Date of Birth	Place of Birth
5ft 8ins	11st 7lbs	6/7/71	Bellshill

	SEASON	CLUB	APP.	GOALS	INTERNATIONAL CAPS	
					APP.	GOALS
CAREER:	88-94	Dundee Utd	78	4		
	94-99	St Johnstone	152	19		

MIDFIELDER
SQUAD NUMBER: 8

The Scottish Premier League has a vision for the future on all fronts - and the information super-highway is no different.

You can log into all the latest news on what's happening in the SPL on www.scotprem.com and the official website also leads you into all the best info on the Top 10 clubs who this season make up our game's elite.

SPL OFFICIAL WEB SITE
www.scotprem.com

PANINI WEB SITE ADDRESS
www.paninigroup.com
FOR MORE EXCITING NEWS ABOUT
PANINIS' SCOTTISH PRODUCTS VISIT OUR WEB SITE

ABERDEEN
Official Web Site
www.afc.co.uk
www.thedons.co.uk

E-Mail Address
talkback@thedons.co.

Unofficial Web Sites
freespace.virgin.net/a.morrison/ajm/afchome.htm
homepages.enterprise.net/howburn/
http://www.raik.demon.co.uk/dons/afc.html

CELTIC
Official Web Site
www.celticfc.co.uk

E-Mail Address
bootroom.comments@celticfc.co.uk

Unofficial Web Sites
www.presence.co.uk/soccer/celtic.html
home.sol.no/~hharsson/celtic.html
www.bhoyzone.com/
http://www.ualberta.ca/~sbo1/myhome9n.htm
members.tripod.com/sm012/home.htm
www.laceltic.com

DUNDEE
Official Web Site
www.dundeefc.co.uk

E-Mail Address
dfc@dundeefc.co.uk

Unofficial Web Sites
www.ianrae.demon.co.uk/dfc/dol_home.htm
www.cee.hw.ac.uk/~estsbn/

DUNDEE UNITED
No official Web site
Unofficial Web Sites
www.geocities.com/Colosseum/3504/dufc.html
www.arabland.demon.co.uk/utd/
www.elder.demon.co.uk/united/index.htm

HEARTS
Official Web Site
www.heartsfc.co.uk

E-Mail Address
live@heartsfc.co.uk

Unofficial Web Sites
ds.dial.pipex.com/town/square/ev90842/hearts.htm
ourworld.compuserve.com/homepages/andy_rainbow_hearts/
www.ednet.co.uk/~ricw/
jambos.aurdev.com/
www.ed.ac.uk/~dwg/

HIBERNIAN
Official Web Site
http://www.hibs.co.uk/

E-Mail Address
club@hibs.co.uk

Unofficial Web Sites
dialspace.dial.pipex.com/cmcc
www.erinweb.org.uk/
www.intasys.com/~gregor/

KILMARNOCK
Official Web Site
www.kilmarnockfc.co.uk

E-Mail Address
kfc@sol.co.uk
No unofficial Web Sites

MOTHERWELL
No official web site
Unofficial Web Sites
www.motherwellfc.mcmail.com/
http://www.geocities.com/Colosseum/Pressbox/7389/

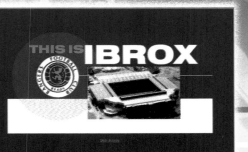

RANGERS
Official Web Site
www.rangers.co.uk

E-Mail Address
dora howie@rangers.co.uk

Unofficial Web Sites
www.x-static.demon.co.uk/rangers/
www.ibrox.mcmail.com/
http://www.ibrox.dircon.co.uk
http://easyweb.easynet.co.uk/~andy.gray/
http://www.geocities.com/Colosseum/Track/7990/
http://www.gla.ac.uk/~ghg1a/Rangers.html

ST. JOHNSTONE
Official Web Site
www.stjohnstonefc.co.uk

Unofficial Web Sites
www.grange.demon.co.uk/saints/sjfc.htm
www.saints.force9.co.uk/abd/index.htm
http://www.grange.demon.co.uk/saints/sjfc.htm
http://www.homeusers.prestel.co.uk/popr/blueheaven/

SO how did you fare with our Old Firm teasers?
Here's the answers to the questions that have kept you guessing.

TRUE OR FALSE

PAGE 20

1 True.
2 True.
3 False it's Alan Stubbs at £3.5m.
4 False.
5 True.

WHO SAID IT?

PAGE 22

1 Dr Jo with some Slovakian wisdom on judging players.
2 Jonathan Gould after a dodgy dye job.
3 Mark Viduka splits for Australia after signing from Croatia Zagreb.
4 Viduka after a stunning debut strike at Morton following stress counselling.
5 Henrik Larsson sparks Celtic joy by agreeing a new four-year deal.

THE TRIVIA QUIZ

PAGE 23

1 Answer: Henrik Larsson and Harald Brattbakk.
2 Answer: Paul McStay, 76 with Scotland.
3 Answer: AS Roma.
4 Answer: Feyenoord.
5 Answer: Croatia Zagreb (Champions League) then FC Zurich (UEFA Cup).

TRUE OR FALSE QUIZ

1 FALSE Answer: 1873.
2 TRUE.
3 FALSE they lost to Bayern Munich in Nuremburg.
4 TRUE.
5 FALSE it was Colin West.

THEY SAID IT

1 Master of understatement Chairman David Murray rates boss Dick Advocaat.
2 Jonatan Johansson buries his past.
3 Lorenzo Amoruso on a downer after a UEFA Cup handball against Parma.
4 Gabriel Amato ponders his future despite a treble in the 5-1 May win at Motherwell.
5 Lionel Charbonnier gets all emotional after Gers fans belt out La Marseillaise.

ARE YOU EAGLE-EYED?

DID you spot him? It's Gabriel Amato against Aberdeen keeper Jim Leighton.

THE TRIVIA QUIZ

1 Answer: Stockholm, Sweden
2 Answer: John Greig
3 Answer: Atletico Madrid
4 Argentina - Holland won the quarter-final 2-1
5 Answer: Claudio Reyna

RSRANGERSRANGERS

HONOURS LIST

1874 Queen's Park	1884 Queen's Park ■	1894 Rangers	1904 Celtic	1914 Celtic	1929 Kilmarnock
1875 Queen's Park	1885 Renton	1895 St Bernard's	1905 Third Lanark	1920 Kilmarnock	1930 Rangers
1876 Queen's Park	1886 Queen's Park	1896 Hearts	1906 Hearts	1921 Partick T	1931 Celtic
1877 Vale of Leven	1887 Hibernian	1897 Rangers	1907 Celtic	1922 Morton	1932 Rangers
1878 Vale of Leven	1888 Renton	1898 Rangers	1908 Celtic	1923 Celtic	1933 Celtic
1879 Vale of Leven ✗	1889 Third Lanark ✓	1899 Celtic	1909 ★	1924 Airdrieonians	1934 Rangers
1880 Queen's Park	1890 Queen's Park	1900 Celtic	1910 Dundee	1925 Celtic	1935 Rangers
1881 Queen's Park ●	1891 Hearts	1901 Hearts	1911 Celtic	1926 St Mirren	1936 Rangers
1882 Queen's Park	1892 Celtic ▲	1902 Hibernian	1912 Celtic	1927 Celtic	1937 Celtic
1883 Dumbarton	1893 Queen's Park	1903 Rangers	1913 Falkirk	1928 Rangers	1938 East Fife

✗ Vale of Leven awarded cup, Rangers failing to appear for replay after 1-1 draw.

● After Dumbarton protested the first game, which Queen's Park won 2-1.

■ Queen's Park awarded cup, Vale of Leven failing to appear

✓ Replay by order of Scottish FA because of playing conditions in first match, won 3-0 by Third Lanark.